Using Science to Develop Thinking Skills at Key Stage 1

Practical resources for gifted and talented learners

Max de Bóo

 David Fulton Publishers

David Fulton Publishers Ltd
The Chiswick Centre, 414 Chiswick High Road, London W4 5TF

www.fultonpublishers.co.uk

First published in Great Britain in 2004 by David Fulton Publishers

Note: The right of Max de Bóo to be identified as the author of this work has been asserted by her in accordance with the Copyright, Designs and Patents Act 1988.

David Fulton Publishers is a division of ITV plc.

British Library Cataloguing in Publication Data
A catalogue record for this book is available from the British Library.

ISBN 1 84312 150 6

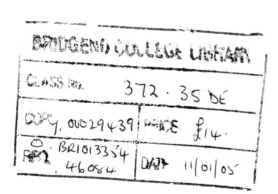
Typeset by RefineCatch Limited, Bungay, Suffolk
Printed and bound in Great Britain

Using Science to Develop Thinking Skills at Key Stage 1

Other titles of interest:

Teaching Thinking Skills Across the Early Years
A practical approach for children aged 4–7
Belle Wallace (Ed.)
1 85346 842 8

Thinking Skills and Early Childhood Education
Patrick J. M. Costello
1 85346 551 8

Creative Science Activity Packs
G. Alan Revill

Includes titles:

- *Rocks*
- *Predators*
- *Minibeasts*
- *Trees and Plants*
- *Materials*
- *Light, Dark and Colour*

Scientific Enquiry Activity Pack
Practical Tasks for Years 3 and 4
John Stringer
1 84312 108 5

Scientific Enquiry Activity Pack
Practical Tasks for Years 5 and 6
John Stringer
1 84312 026 7

Contents

Autumn is ....

Autumn is when leaves fall off the trees,
twirling and swirling gracefully,
turning brown, gold, yellow, and orange.
As they slowly start to fall they go spotty,
wrinkly, curly, crispy, spiky,
and go into lots of strange shapes.
Autumn is when the trees
curl up in monstrous shapes,
trees swish as they catch the wind.
As they come alive
clawing the houses in terror,
rottening brown.
Autumn is when the first winds begin to blow.
Jack Frost spreads the first frost upon the autumn morning.
Fog spreads on the crunchy leaves.
Animals flowers and trees disappear for hibernation.

(by Frances, aged 6 years)

Zebra

The zebra runs swiftly tail held high
running so proudly.
Its black and white stripes camouflage
in the tall green grass.
It gallops along with pounding hooves
looking for the tallest piece of grass to eat.
It sees the grass, gobbles it up and starts looking for another.
When it's finished eating
it gallops along looking for the rest of the herd.
It has a velvety muzzle that touches
as it goes along with the herd.

(by Jessica, 6 years)

Introduction

Identifying scientifically gifted children

Five Reception children (four- to five-years-old), were being interviewed on their thinking about 'heat', using a picture of a volcano to initiate the discussion.

Teacher with Kylie and Sheena

Teacher:	I wonder what made the volcano get so hot?
Kylie and Sheena:	Fire.
Sheena:	And smoke.
Teacher:	I see what you mean. And is there any way of making the volcano cool down, do you think?
Kylie:	Water!
Sheena:	Firemen . . .
Kylie:	You could get a hose pipe.
Teacher:	A hose pipe?
Kylie:	Yeah, 'cos some pipes are really big and the firemen can stretch it right over to the volcano.

Teacher with Tony and Alex

Teacher:	I wonder what made the volcano get so hot?
Tony:	Well, Jesus done it. I mean God.
Teacher:	Yes, I see. Is there any way of making the volcano cool down, do you think?
Alex:	Only from the sky.

> **Teacher with Sanjiv**
>
> Teacher: Do you know where the volcano gets its heat from?
>
> Sanjiv: Yes. When the Earth plates stuck . . . touch together.
>
> Teacher: Why, what does that do?
>
> Sanjiv: It makes the heat . . . the Earth plates push together . . . and then the fire comes out.
>
> Teacher: Is there any way of stopping the Earth plates pushing together?
>
> Sanjiv: No.

We meet children like Sanjiv rarely; his responses are unusual and exceptional. We meet children like Kylie and Sheena more often; they draw conclusions using cause and effect and are potentially high achievers. We meet children like Tony and Alex most frequently; their answers a mixture of the subjective and objective, although they are capable of responding with higher order thinking if given enough stimuli and regular challenges.

The definitions of gifted and talented children generally used for inspection purposes by Ofsted (Office for Standards in Education) define these children as those who show higher ability in all or some areas of the curriculum. The statement is clarified by defining 'gifted' children as showing high ability or potential in academic subjects and 'talented' children showing high ability or potential in the expressive, creative arts or sports. Researchers and government guidelines work on the principle that there are probably 5 to 10 per cent of school children who can be described as gifted and talented and a further 10 per cent who are very high achievers. In Wales (ACCAC) Awdurdod Cymwyskron Cwricwlwm ac Asesu Cymru, the standard definition is that 20 per cent of children are 'more able and talented' and the Scottish Office agrees with these notional figures. However, it is often confusing to classify children, especially from four to seven years, so we need to keep an open mind and assume a figure of about 15 to 20 per cent of highly talented children. We can proceed on the assumption that in an average group of children there are likely to be some high achievers and occasionally, an exceptionally gifted or talented child.

The difficulty in identifying young children with high ability arises because their cognitive, emotional and physical development is uneven 'and the more gifted a child is the more pronounced the unevenness [can] be' (Silverman 1993). However, Silverman identified some of the characteristics that help us identify these children:

Intellectual characteristics

- exceptional reasoning ability
- rapid learning rate
- complex thought processes
- early moral concern
- powers of concentration
- divergent thinking/creativity
- capacity for reflection
- intellectual curiosity
- facility with abstraction
- vivid imagination
- passion for learning
- analytical thinking
- keen sense of justice

Personality characteristics

- insightfulness
- need for precision/logic
- perfectionism
- sensitivity/empathy
- intensity
- acute self-awareness
- questioning of rules/authority

- need to understand
- need for mental stimulation
- excellent sense of humour
- perseverance
- non-conformity
- tendency towards introversion

Some of the children we teach will show some or many of these characteristics. However, the most important thing about teaching able young children is that, first and foremost, they are *children*. Their social and emotional needs are similar to their peers. The fact that they are highly intelligent can be daunting enough to make us concentrate on their *abilities*, as we might focus on a person's disabilities, rather than on them as a person.

Sanjiv

At one time I was asking Sanjiv [the gifted child mentioned earlier] his thoughts about candles and melting, using a tape recorder. After a few minutes, he got fed up talking about the burning candle and wanted to take the tape recorder apart. When I protested, he began speaking in a very quiet whisper. 'Now the tape recorder can't hear me anyway,' he said. And smiled.

The *official* requirement to 'identify giftedness' is not easily satisfied; in young children, ability is often latent and will develop in the quality of the provision made. It is not helped if those talented children are also impatient, demanding, disrespectful or short-tempered with us or the other children. The world of the gifted and talented child must present a great deal of confusion – 'Why don't grown-ups think as quickly as I do? Why do other children offer silly (naïve) ideas in response to questions? Why do I have to work so slowly when I can do 100 things twice as fast as the others?' Koshy (2002: 109) stated that able children underachieve for the following reasons:

- Frustration – bored with the content on offer
- Resentment – prefer to read instead of listen or do instead of talk
- Fear of failure – perfectionism or nothing
- Bored with the topic – need stimuli
- Low level of intellectual stimulation
- Hiding real ability to obtain acceptance from peers
- Frustrated by and resentful of low level of ability of peers

This negative behaviour can mask their ability – although there can be no excuse for disrupting lessons. Young gifted children need support – they will not thrive all on their own. They can help other children some of the time and acquire social skills but this should not dominate their experience. Furthermore, in an ordinary classroom setting, many other children require our support also. Appeals to the local education authority for psychologists to assess gifted children can take time, as these psychologists have a big caseload. My experience of this process includes waiting a whole year for a six-year-old gifted child to be assessed, and then the test was incomplete.

> ### Noah
> The local authority psychologist came to assess six-year-old Noah. After 45 minutes of the IQ test, Noah got bored. He said 'I don't want to do any more!' After pleas to stay, he carried on for five minutes. Then the dinner bell rang. 'I want my dinner now,' declared Noah and walked out. His IQ at the walking out stage was 187!

Given the difficulties in identifying scientifically gifted children, this book is designed as follows:

- First, the book offers strategies for teaching all children who may yet be recognised as very capable learners in science. When young children are offered stimulating opportunities and challenging questions in situations where they feel safe and confident, they can perform at a much higher level than previously expected (de Bóo, unpublished research, 1989–1995). That is, with the supportive 'scaffolding' described by Bruner (1968), children's learning advances into what Vygotsky (1986) called the 'zone of proximal development' (see page 12).

- Secondly, this book offers science activities and teaching strategies for the high achievers – the 15 to 20 per cent of children who are bright, open-minded, quick and enthusiastic learners.

- Finally, this book offers teaching material to address the needs of the few children that might be assessed as exceptionally gifted and talented in science.

Some children may lack high ability in literacy and numeracy but still shine in science. There seems to be no correlation between high-fliers in English and maths and children who show talent in the knowledge and understanding of science (O'Brien 1998). This has implications for classroom organisation and grouping (see pages, 13, 24). Qualter (1996: 44) states that 'ability is determined by where the child is and what the child's capacity for learning is' but factors such as motivation, personality and home background have a significant effect on converting a child's potential into performance.

Involving and valuing parents

Most of us as parents are programmed to think of our children as potentially high achievers in some form or another. And so we should. However, this can mean that information gathered from parents can be rather subjective.

Nevertheless, it is very important to gain as much information from parents as possible to identify needs and interests as well as abilities. Interviews prior to and during the early school years are best focused on the individual children, their interests and out-of-school pursuits. O'Brien (1998: 3) suggests subjects for discussion could include the following:

- What types of activities get the children excited and how do they behave?
- What questions do they ask? Do they use language that is mature for their age?
- What is their reaction when they are given an answer to a question?
- What books do the children read, how do they view reading and to what purpose do they use reading?
- What types of television programme do the children watch?
- What sort of games do the children enjoy playing: e.g. computer games, board games, football, dancing [involving logic, strategies, rules, individuality, co-operation]?
- What websites on the Internet do the children visit?
- Do the children like to take things apart to determine how they work?
- When involved in an activity do the children concentrate for long periods of time and persevere to solve problems?
- When working on a task do the children work independently or do they need supervision?
- What is the reaction of the children if you take them to an interactive science exhibition or museum?

Teachers can help parents to gain a wider perspective by comparing their children's achievements with their peers and against national standards. Parents need to be made aware of the importance of the social development of the more able child. This is the age of communication and poor social skills can limit the opportunities of even the ablest child. The day of the scientific genius working in isolation is past. Nowadays, cutting-edge scientific research is carried out in hi-tech laboratories, usually in teams, with government or corporate sponsorship, building on the work of scientists across the world (e.g. Watson and Crick, and DNA). Able children need to learn to communicate positively and effectively. Parents may need advice in *how* to encourage their children's capabilities. After-school activities can be very beneficial but able children also need time to just 'play', whether at the computer, watching television or kicking a ball around with other children. In surveying parental provision. Ofsted inspectors found that sometimes adult-provided activities reduced children's opportunities for play and discouraged communication and imagination. Finding the balance is crucial – over-stimulation can frustrate a child just as much as lack of stimulus!

Provision and the role of the teacher

Like all human talents, scientific ability can be cultivated or destroyed. Able pupils need stimulating provision that allows them to develop at their own pace. Ofsted repeatedly highlights the lack of provision for able pupils in ordinary classes. The government White Paper (DfEE 1997) stated that encouraging the more able was so important that they want every school and local education authority to identify and plan how it will support gifted and talented children. HMI Mackintosh (Ofsted 1994: 13) reported that 'there is clear evidence that focusing sharply on what the most able can achieve raises the expectations generally, because ... it involves consideration of the organisation and management of teaching and learning.' We need a curriculum and assessment framework which achieves this, and one that makes the provision relevant and appropriate for younger children. 'Such provision should be integral to the school curriculum, not an "add-on" extra' (David Miliband, Education Minister, interviewed on *Today*, BBC Radio 4, 31 March 2003).

Translating government directives into action in the classroom requires the vital support of head teachers (Ofsted 1993). At the classroom level, teachers have to deliver daily differentiated programmes of learning when there are likely to be:

- children with special educational needs (SEN) who have difficulty in reaching basic targets,
- children of average ability who will achieve national standards, or
- children who are very able.

Time is limited for focused interactions between teachers and pupils on a one-to-one or one-to-two basis. The 'need to achieve basic standards' is perceived as more important than the 'need to fulfil potential' and as a result, gifted and talented children often receive less focused interaction time with the teacher or stimulating challenges than they need. In their own way, able children have 'special educational needs'. These children can become frustrated with a curriculum content which is achievable for them in half the time that other children take, with perhaps only 10 per cent of their attention. Frustrated children can be disruptive: behaviourally or intellectually manipulative. The most able children need stimulating challenges with adult guides who rejoice in their talents.

Teachers are at the front line of teaching and learning and need support. There is some overlap in roles and responsibilities but there are some areas we can define as follows.

School level

At the school level, co-ordinators for science and/or co-ordinators for gifted and talented children should:

- use national criteria (e.g. curriculum guidance for the UK: England, Wales, Northern Ireland and Scotland) and staff discussions to devise a policy to identify and cater for the most able children
- agree progression for able pupils to explore aspects of the science curriculum before their chronological peers
- expect high achievement by identifying in the Scheme of Work the range of outcomes for differing abilities

- agree procedures for positive assessment and constructive comments
- agree procedures for collecting portfolios of exemplar work from able pupils and sharing this information with other staff and with parents
- create a school ethos where success and failure are acknowledged as a positive part of the learning process
- provide enthusiastic support for science at school level in extra-curricular activities (e.g. science clubs, homework, SATIS-style work [Science and Technology in Society, Stringer/SATIS (1996) available at www.ase.org.uk], British Association National Science Week [the-ba.org.uk/nsw]) which promote different thinking from school science and the involvement of interested parents
- allocate funding for science resources to extend the most able (including books and ICT) and train colleagues in their use, if necessary
- identify and monitor health and safety issues
- identify level of language, use of scientific vocabulary and a range of recording and presentation methods
- create links with outside agencies such as local PhD students or scientists working in industry
- make regular provision of opportunities and funding for training Co-ordinators and class teachers with able pupils.

Classroom level

At the classroom level the class teacher should:

- identify children who are very able and those who may have potential for higher achievement using agreed strategies
- set clearly identified learning objectives and share these with the children
- identify key progressive concepts and use these to plan extension and enrichment activities
- engage with parents in the dialogue of effective provision for their children
- motivate children with good quality, safe, stimulating and developmental resources (from handlenses to stopwatches)
- identify scientific vocabulary and a range of recording methods
- plan practical activities for all children but ensure such activities offer wider opportunities for the able child and divergent thinker
- use open-ended, person-centred questions to encourage creative thinking skills (see page 16)
- encourage children to ask their own questions and share or take responsibility for designing their own investigations to answer these
- provide opportunities and resources for independent learning by children's own projects, ICT and other recording tasks

- promote scientific understanding by using models and analogies, and encourage children to use different strategies (e.g. 3-D models, drama, ICT) to explain scientific phenomena
- encourage children's progress and self-esteem by giving positive feedback and constructive criticism
- encourage children to evaluate their own learning by considering what they have learnt compared with what they knew at the start
- evaluate the teaching strategies they have used and their effectiveness.

How children learn science

What *is* science? Science is both a body of knowledge and a way of investigating our world. The scientific process is a questioning, testing process that challenges assumptions and preconceptions. In science, the body of 'knowledge' is regarded as temporary – it is what we believe to be true right now but in the future it may need to be refined, modified or replaced by more accurate 'knowledge'. For teaching and learning purposes, there is a consensus of opinion on identifying and setting out scientific skills, attitudes and knowledge as learning objectives (National Curriculum [England], DFEE/QCA 1999; Environmental Studies [Scotland], Scottish Office Education Department 2000; ACCAC [Wales]):

- Knowledge of
    - Life processes and living things – natural or environmental science
    - Materials and their properties – the way materials behave
    - Physical processes – electricity, forces and motion, light and sound, Earth science
- Skills of scientific enquiry – careful observation, questioning, predicting, testing things out, coming to conclusions, suggesting explanations or hypotheses, evaluating the methods used, communicating to others
- Attitudes such as curiosity, perseverance, open-mindedness, co-operation, critical thinking, caring for the environment, sensitivity to living things, and responsibility for one's behaviour.

Children are more likely to be tested on their scientific knowledge than on their skills, attitudes and understanding. Skills and attitudes are best revealed when children engage in a hands-on investigation in which we can see them observing closely, showing curiosity, offering explanations, co-operating with others or behaving safely. Understanding is better shown when children are asked to apply their knowledge in a new, problem-solving situation. Children who show talent in science may be less confident in literacy and numeracy. Curriculum constraints over the past two decades have reduced the amount of time spent on practical science and this has had a detrimental effect on children who shine at science or learn best in a hands-on, tactile–kinaesthetic way.

Learning in science is not successful if reduced to learning by rote and recalled for a paper and pencil test. Scientific thinking is a dynamic mixture of logic and creativity and takes place when something is *happening* or *has happened* (i.e. a practical exploration/investigation) and when we *imagine something happening* (i.e. predictions/hypotheses/thought experiments). For example, in the vignette below the children commented on what was happening then and there, on what might have happened and why. They imagined what they might see when they turned the fish over, wondered what might have made the fish like it was, and why. Vicki imagined what might happen to the fish if it had eyes on both sides (that is, she was evaluating the functioning of the fish).

A visit to the fishmongers

A group of six- and seven-year-old children were visiting the fishmongers and looking closely at the white underside of a sole (no eyes visible – both on the other side of its body).

Teacher:	I wonder where the fish's eyes are?
Mei Ling:	It hasn't got any.
Paul:	They've been cut out by the fishmonger.
Jamie:	It doesn't need eyes.
Vicki:	Maybe it finds its way by smelling.
Jamie:	Naw, you can't smell nothing in the sea.
Paul:	You don't know that.
Vicki:	Maybe it can hear its way by listening.
Teacher:	Do you think it's white on both sides?
All children:	Yes

The fish is turned over.

Mei Ling:	Oh, it's grey . . .
Paul:	Oh, I can see its eye.
Jamie:	It's got one eye.
Mei Ling:	No, it's got two eyes – look . . . black ones.
Vicki:	Why has this fish got orange spots on?
Jamie:	Why are they so flat?
Teacher:	Why do you think?
Jamie:	When they lie in the sand, nobody can see them.
Vicki:	They can hide in the sand like camouflage.
Mei Ling:	Somebody might step on them.
Paul:	There's nobody walking down there.
Mei Ling:	Well, people go underwater swimming sometimes . . . deep sea divers like that film last night on the telly.
Vicki:	Do you know something – if this fish had eyes on each side like ordinary fish, the bottom eye would get full of sand.

Science tests are becoming more balanced in valuing 'knowing how to' skills although there is still too little emphasis on scientific attitudes (curiosity, self-criticism). The children in the vignette above showed great curiosity and were quite comfortable with criticism of their ideas. We need to focus on such skills and 'learning how to learn' as this reduces the domination of subject content and nurtures good learning habits for the future.

Effective teaching strategies

Children's learning is optimised when we:

1. provide a safe but stimulating environment
2. establish positive relationships with the children
3. provide cognitive challenges
4. give support to scaffold the children's development
5. differentiate for individual children.

1. Providing a safe, stimulating environment

A safe environment is one in which the children's physical and emotional well-being is safeguarded. There are recognisable and consistent classroom rules, varying from 'not running in the classroom' to 'taking turns to speak in the plenary'. Children need to feel valued, regardless of their strengths and weaknesses, successes and failures. Such an environment will offer opportunities to work in small groups and independently, in both formal and exploratory activities. A stimulating environment offers interesting resources and activities (handlenses and microscopes, unusual shells and autumn leaves, burning candles) as well as cognitive challenges and opportunities to solve problems. In such an environment, not only do we cater for able children but well-motivated children of average ability can often achieve as much as the very able. Chief HMI David Bell stated repeatedly in TV and radio interviews in 2003 that a flexible timetable and a willingness to let pupils experiment motivates and inspires young children, fostering curiosity, play and imagination.

2. Establishing positive relationships with the children

> 'The curriculum is so much raw material, but warmth is the vital element for the growing plant and the soul of the child.'
>
> Carl Jung (1875–1961)

Positive personal relationships are crucial in promoting young children's learning – they *'form the matrix within which* [the child's] *learning takes place'* (Donaldson 1987: 88). The Lifelong Learning Foundation (2000) identified six aspects of learning: 'the ability to relate to a teacher, confidence that you can progress, ability to make connections, curiosity, creativity and the ability to talk about learning', but emphasised that 'the most important thing [about children learning effectively] appeared to be the quality of the learning relationship with the teacher'.

Face-to-face communication is especially important – tone of voice, body language and choice of language influence pupil learning as well as the establishment of classroom rules and personal relationships.

Regular, constructive verbal interactions between pupils and teachers would include the teacher clarifying the learning objectives for the children, together with regular consulting and giving the children postive feedback. In a positive atmosphere where children's questions are encouraged, welcomed and valued, they quickly learn that question-asking is a positive way of 'finding answers' (Tizard and Hughes 1984), as well as referring to parents, books and the Internet. Young children who lack confidence may misunderstand instructions and remain silent rather than ask questions to clarify the tasks (Cosgrove and Patterson 1977) and even think less of themselves (which will mask any potential talent).

Positive dialogue with children needs to reflect a two-way honesty. Telling children explicitly when they have or have not been understood is an effective way of encouraging children to articulate what they know (Robinson and Robinson 1981). One way of doing this is to state clearly: 'I'm not sure what you mean. Can you explain it to me again, please.' Another way is to repeat a child's statement in the form of a question, as in the vignette on page 1: (*Kylie: You could get a hose pipe. Teacher: A hose pipe?*). Both strategies give a positive message to the child – they say 'I am interested in what you have to say. I value your ideas'. This kind of response puts the responsibility on the child to articulate their thinking more clearly – they respond by clarifying and expanding their ideas. Thus, saying things aloud is an act of learning itself. It also gives other children time to listen again, have more thinking time, reach an understanding and offer their own responses.

The relative values of group work will be discussed later (page 13), but at the end of the day it is 'not the style of class teaching that is the crucial factor but the quality of teacher–pupil interactions' (Galton *et al.* 1980).

3. Providing cognitive challenges

There are four discrete stages of learning:

Unconscious incompetence	*The child is unaware that she doesn't know*
	= a comfortable state
Conscious incompetence	*The child now knows that she doesn't know*
	= discomfort/temporary loss of self-esteem/possible frustration
Unconscious competence	*The child does not realise that she knows yet*
	= discomfort but self-aware and learning
Conscious competence	*The child now knows that she knows*
	= confidence in knowing

Children cannot advance cognitively without some form of challenge that results in internal conflict or 'knowing that they don't know'. Cognitive challenges are sometimes misconstrued as simply attempting higher knowledge targets in national curricula (e.g. targeting higher National Curriculum levels). Rather, cognitive challenges are better set within the initial activity as well as enrichment and extension activities. The latter will consolidate understanding and offer a wider curriculum more appropriate for a young child. The best cognitive challenges are not over-demanding – there is a dynamic relationship between comfort and challenge (Merry 1998: 116). Pupils can be set problems to solve, cross-curricular activities and research into books or the Internet, all of which value the fact that they are still young children. Most of all, cognitive challenges require effective questions (see page 16).

Sometimes, gifted and talented children find it hard to accept that there is something they don't know. They have been absorbing information at such a rate that they usually know more than their peers and occasionally more than some of the grown-ups around them. For example, four-year-old Sanjiv (page 2) knew something about plate tectonics (the theory that the Earth's crust consists of continental plates and where these are growing [the Atlantic Ocean Ridge], or being subducted [near Japan], there is volcanic activity). When I responded with enthusiasm, he guessed that I might know something more than him about the subject (not a lot). He waved his hand dismissively at me and said, 'Don't tell me that!' A balance is needed between acknowledging our own lack of knowledge and demonstrating greater knowledge and understanding.

Nevertheless, occasional failure or 'not knowing' is important for able children. Diane Hofkins, reporting on the National Primary Study (TES 2003) stated that 'gifted children need the chance to fail in an atmosphere where they can work on challenging tasks without losing too much self-esteem'. Children who are perceived as super-clever or 'always right' can be ostracised or avoided by classmates.

4. Scaffolding the children's development/working in groups

Vygotsky (1986) argued that children have a capacity for performing at a more advanced level than they may show. He called this the 'zone of proximal development'. The zone of proximal development 'refers to the gap that exists for an individual child or adult between what he is able to do alone and what he can achieve with help from one more knowledgeable or skilled than himself' (Wood 1992: 24). Most teachers now agree that children's learning is achieved co-operatively in formal and informal ways with support from more knowledgeable peers or siblings, parents, grandparents, friends, acquaintances and teachers. It does appear, however, that some children have larger zones of proximal development than others even when their existing levels of performance are similar. 'Scaffolding' is the term subsequently coined by Bruner (1968) to describe the support given to a child to help him progress from his existing level of performance into his potential zone of proximal development.

So what constitutes such 'scaffolding'? In science, opportunities for practical hands-on experiences will support developmental thinking. Cognitive challenges and effective questioning (page 16) will encourage communication and thinking skills. The use of different teaching styles to correspond to children's learning styles (visual, auditory, tactile–kinaesthetic) will optimise children's performance (Merry 1978). Role modelling the kind of behaviour that we wish to encourage acts as scaffolding:

listening

questioning

encouraging children's own questions

showing one's own curiosity and enthusiasm

directing attention to features, words and ideas

amplifying what the children say

offering strategies such as analogies to aid understanding

giving approval

suggesting modifications

giving children space and time to try things out without our intervention

providing opportunities to follow up their own interests (projects)

making children aware of their own thinking skills

acknowledging when we ourselves 'don't know'.

Gifted children can, of course, help to scaffold other children's learning. They could be partnered with another child (Tony Gardiner 2003) and although this means that the more able pupils progress more slowly, they will benefit hugely from working with another and from the opportunity to explain (thereby taking some of the strain off the teacher). Varying the way children are grouped can actively support the able child (Table 1.1).

Table 1.1 Grouping: the advantages and disadvantages

Type of group	Advantages	Disadvantages
Friendship groups	Develop social skills, opportunities for different roles (group leader, assistant), opportunity to share different knowledge or ideas during the activity and in the plenary.	Able children can get bored and argumentative, want to do other things, want to tell the answers too soon.
Ability group	Opportunities for concentrated work, able children can develop more advanced ideas for investigating and share new ideas in plenary sessions.	Needs careful planning and resources, can distract other children and cause resentment.
Individual work in ones or twos	Ideal for extension and enrichment work. Caters for differences in children's performances and abilities. Less equipment and resources needed. Can generate enthusiasm and capitalise on able children's interests.	Can cause resentment unless all children have opportunities to work in this way from time to time. Can be tricky choosing appropriate partners. Need to find time for feedback and share results of individual research.

Above all, we need to remember that the most important resource for the child is the adult: the parent and teacher. Keep an open mind, be flexible and be ready to adapt ideas or material to suit the child as well as establishing routines and expectations – a teacher has needs too!

5. Differentiation

Differentiation is the process of identifying, with each learner, the most effective strategies for achieving agreed targets. The needs of the individual child may be many and varied. Silverman (1993) described the development of cognitive, emotional and physical factors in the young child as 'asynchronous', that is, developing at different rates. For example, there is often a mismatch between cognitive and physical development. 'This creates inner tension . . . [which] can lead to frustration, a tension made more difficult as young children change at a faster rate than older children' (Qualter 1996: 16).

Planned differentiation takes time but is effective and also provides material for assessing children's performance. We need to be prepared for the children who are able to go further – to find time for them, and be ready to justify our decisions to parents and school managers. Children need activities and challenges that are relevant to them and their experience, their current interests and their family backgrounds. Differentiation motivates children, maximises their learning and facilitates good teaching (Sylva 1994). A child who enjoys learning is 'learning how to learn'.

We can differentiate for the more able children in the following ways (based on Keogh *et al.* 2002).

Outcome

- Clearly targeting appropriate science concepts and skills
- Using more advanced methods of recording – written, ICT, maths
- Setting individual projects to maximise children's interests

The degree of challenge

- Assigning tasks requiring different levels of skill, knowledge and understanding
- Planning tasks that contain an element of problem-solving
- Using children's own ideas for investigations
- Asking open-ended questions

Secondary tasks/extension and enrichment

- Planning and preparing resources for additional activities and research

Using more sophisticated resources and equipment

- Training children in the use of equipment

Using more advanced language and vocabulary

- Introducing and using scientific vocabulary
- Varying the level of literacy demand, or how the activity is presented

Open-ended questioning and other questions

- Targeting questions to match individual children's background and potential ability

Expectation of support for their peers

- Expectation of collaborative work with other children as leaders, shared assistants, researchers, presenters

Thinking skills

Nowadays there is little need to argue the case for teaching children how to think. Learning to think is as important as learning how to read, how to count, how to catch a ball. Learning to think teaches us how to learn and how to think for ourselves. Young children think both subjectively and objectively, although always creatively if given the opportunity. As we grow older, our thinking usually becomes more objective, although in truth, adult thinking is always fundamentally subjective, set in a context of individual, personal and cultural experience and is never value-free.

In many ways, thinking skills (Bloom 1956) are synonymous with scientific skills (de Bóo 1999), as shown in Table 1.2.

Thinking 'out loud' has a social and communicative dimension as well as regulating a child's own thinking. Thinking out loud transforms the way children learn, understand and respond to other children. Establishing a stimulating but safe environment and using effective questioning techniques

Table 1.2 The level of thinking involved in different scientific skills

Scientific skill	Level of thinking	Example
Observation	Lower order	Description (*It's red.*)
Asking questions (i)	Lower order	Seeking information (*Is it a . . . ?*)
Asking questions (ii)	**Higher order**	Seeing patterns (*What will happen if . . . ?*)
Classification (i)	Lower order	Simple patterns (*all red*)
Classification (ii)	**Higher order**	More complex patterns (*alive/not alive*)
Predictions	**Higher order**	Imaginative/Creative (*It will get bigger.*)
Drawing conclusions (i)	Lower order	Descriptive (*It disappeared.*)
Drawing conclusions (ii)	**Higher order**	Cause and effect (*The heat made it go . . . .*)
Drawing conclusions (iii)	**Higher order**	Analogies (*It's like a clock.*)
Hypotheses/Explanations	**Higher order**	Imaginative/Creative (*I think it's the Sun doing it./It finds its way by smelling.*)
Evaluation	**Higher order**	Critical reflection/Problem solving (*It would be better if . . ./I could find out on the web . . ./I could make it go better if I . . .*)
Metacognitive	**Higher order**	Conscious self-processing (*I don't know – I never thunk it before.*)

ensures that even the youngest child can show higher order thinking and responses.

Effective questioning

Generally speaking, there are two types of question: closed or subject-centred and open-ended or person-centred. For example:

Closed	Open-ended
Has it dissolved yet?	What do you notice about the liquid?
What do we call a tree that loses its leaves in winter?	What do you think will happen to the trees in the cold weather?
Can you see the blue flame? What is that called?	What do you notice about the flame? Anything else? Or?
Do you remember how to do it?	What made you think that?

Teachers ask a lot questions. Good questions can stimulate thinking by making cognitive demands on children (Tizard and Hughes 1984). In the past, most of the questions asked by teachers in the classroom required nothing more than automatic or low level responses (Galton *et al.* 1980). Some of these questions are necessarily limited – aimed at class control, gaining information, showing interest or checking that instructions have been understood. Of the rest, 95 per cent of teachers' questions were 'closed', requiring one-word (yes/no) or factual answers or recall of the teacher's statements (Wood 1992). Only 5 per cent of all teachers' questions were open-ended. Teachers do usually ask questions to which they already know the answers – safe but placing no value on the children's thinking skills (Barnes *et al.* 1986).

However, closed questions can generate anxiety in children and loss of self-confidence (not knowing the 'right' answer) and stifle enquiries. Children's responses to open-ended questions cannot be predicted and teachers may not know how to deal with this – a risky business! Nevertheless, pupil achievement is higher when children encounter open-ended questions with a greater cognitive demand (Redfield and Rousseau 1981). My research over several years showed a much greater number of creative, thoughtful responses when the emphasis is shifted from recalling relevant but abstract knowledge to the child's personal thinking or experience. I found that the open-ended questions shown in Table 1.3 encourage thinking skills and give children the opportunity to show their wide-ranging knowledge and enthusiasms.

The are two key words in the questions shown in Table 1.3: '*you*' and '*think*'. These questions are open-ended, person-centred. Of course, the responses still give recalled knowledge but so much more. Apart from making the activity more relevant to each individual child, we gain information for formative assessments of what the children know and what we need to do next. For example, in the vignette below, one could not have predicted the responses from Albert or Kiana – showing their awareness of the speed of sound or the mixing of gases!

Table 1.3 How open-ended questions encourage thinking skills (de Bóo 1999)

Type of question	Responses
What do you notice about . . . ?	Descriptive observations
What can you tell me about . . . ?	Inviting recalled information but content chosen by the children
What does it remind you of?	Seeing patterns/analogies
Which things do you think belong together? Why do you think that?	Seeing patterns/classifying and creative explanations
What do you think will happen next?	Creative predictions
What happened after you did that?	Descriptive reasoning/cause and effect/conclusions
Why do you think that happened? I wonder why it did that?	Creative hypotheses/explanations
Do you think you could do it differently?	Evaluation/reflective analysis
I wonder what made you think that?	Reflective self-awareness/metacognition
Anything else? Or?	Neutral/Inviting more of the responses listed above

---

Albert and Kiana

Exploring the nature of sounds with a group of six- to seven-year-olds, a pin was dropped at a little distance from the children:

Teacher: What do you notice about the sound?

Albert: This ear could hear it first.

Kiana: Sound goes fast, doesn't it?

Then a balloon was popped:

Teacher: Why do you think it made that sound?

Kiana: The air's waiting to come out.

Jordan: Yes, it wants to come out quick.

Albert: Then the air from it [the balloon] will mix up and be the same as the air outside.

Questions can be asked prior to and during science enquiries, and later in the plenary. It is always important to allow children time to think after asking the questions – allowing time to respond in science activities can improve learning. In reality, there is unlikely to be a silent pause very often, as open-ended questions inspire children to respond easily, giving space to those children who need more time to think. In any dialogue, we need to value cultural and gender differences, individual needs and interests.

Open-ended questions allow *all* children to answer successfully but give opportunities for able children to reveal their thinking and knowledge at higher levels. High level responses from able children can have different effects on the other children:

- some children do not understand the responses but accept them positively
- some children may 'switch off' and stop listening temporarily
- some children are stimulated into higher order thinking themselves.

So the overall effect on other children is positive most of the time. However, a balance must be kept – it is all too seductive to engage in lengthy dialogues with the more able while other children are getting bored. Time has to be found at other times for more intensive dialogue with able children in smaller groups or one-to-one. Even brief interactions of higher order thinking will motivate gifted children and help them sustain their on-task concentration (Naylor and Keogh 2000).

Assessment and keeping records

Teachers observe and assess children's development on a daily basis: their use of language, motor skills, understanding of number, social skills etc. The more informed we are about a child's starting point, the better our provision of appropriate tasks and support. In science, younger children are not given national tests. We rely upon the assessment of each class teacher to assess children in science from four to seven years. We need to assess different kinds of knowledge:

- knowing that (knowledge concepts, e.g. ice melts into water)
- knowing why (understanding, e.g. heat causes changes in materials, such as solid ice melting into liquid water)
- knowing how to (Sc1 skills, e.g. predicting that ice will melt from the outside; measuring how long it will take to melt etc.)
- knowing that we know or don't know (attitudes, e.g. curiosity, behaving safely, and metacognition, e.g. 'I know how to do it').

(de Bóo 1999)

Summative assessment is useful prior to the start of a new learning unit and at the end of the unit. Formative assessment is the ongoing observation and diagnosis of children's strengths and weaknesses. There are a range of methods which can be used to assess and record children's learning in science, as shown in Table 1.4.

It can be seen from Table 1.4 that some of the methods of assessment provide some form of permanent evidence while others (e.g. verbal responses) are ephemeral and will need to be noted down as soon as possible after the discussion or event. An audio tape recorder is a great asset in supporting recalled discussions and children become accustomed to its use, as well as enjoying listening to themselves sometimes! Evidence of all kinds is invaluable for keeping class and individual records of attainment and building up a child's profile. In particular, the evidence helps to identify children with special scientific ability. Most important of all, decisions about what and how to assess depend on clarifying the learning objectives.

Table 1.4 Advantages and disadvantages of different methods of assessment

Method of assessment	Advantages	Disadvantages
Observation of children's performance (e.g. Mal tested the paper three times without prompting, 'to be sure'.)		
Carry out during a practical exploration or investigation, whether individually or in groups. Use another observer, or tape recorder, or make notes later.	*Vitally important* to obtain information about children's scientific skills and attitudes, e.g. 'fair testing' and curiosity.	Difficult to take notes on the spot or recall and make notes later.
Children's verbal responses		
(a) responding to a teacher's questions (b) asking their own questions (c) volunteering information and ideas (d) conversations with other children (e) responding to concept cartoons (see page 28) (f) children's analogies (e.g. 'The candle is going like my ice lolly, drippy down and melting' and the discussion about salt in Figure 1.1.)	*Very valuable* for gaining information about children's conceptual knowledge and understanding, scientific skills and attitudes, and thinking processes.	Not always easy to remember 'who said what' – use recall and tape recorders.
Children's drawings		
(a) observational drawings of objects (see Figure 1.2a and b) or investigation then and there (b) drawings of recalled objects and the investigation results (c) drawing a prediction of what might happen (see Figure 1.3), instead of a written prediction (d) drawings of imaginary objects or phenomena or sources of materials	*Important,* as can give information about children's knowledge, skills of observing and predicting, and individual interests and creativity. Useful in providing a record of some permanency. Photocopy the original for the Pupil Profile.	
Written work – by hand or using ICT (see Figures 1.4 and 1.5)		
(a) children's own question (b) suggested answers to questions (c) narrating a sequential account of a science enquiry (d) recording the outcomes only (e) recording the children's explanations only (f) writing an imaginary story about the science being studied (e.g. The cress that grew too large!) (g) writing the outcome of individual or group research	*Valuable* in giving information about children's conceptual knowledge and understanding. Can be used to assess children's creative ideas. Useful in providing a record of some permanency. Photocopy and keep the original or a photocopy in the Pupil Profile.	Not so easy to assess children's skills and attitudes. Requires pupils who are confident in writing skills and vocabulary.
Numerical work – by hand or using ICT		
(a) record of collected data/numbers (b) records of measurements taken (c) simple bar charts	*Valuable* in giving information about children's scientific knowledge and mathematical skills.	Understanding cannot be easily assessed without verbal or written

Table 1.4 Continued

Method of assessment	Advantages	Disadvantages
(d) more complex graphs, e.g. line graphs, scattergraphs, pie charts	Use to provide a permanent record or the Pupil Profile (or a photocopy).	interpretations of the data/graphs.
3-D models and collages		
(e.g. representations of worms and beetles in modelling clay, bubble wrap with black dots for frogspawn)	*Valuable* in giving information about children's understanding of a scientific concept or phenomenon.	Not easy to retain as permanent evidence. Take photographs for the Pupil Profile.
Drama		
(a) mime, e.g. the conductivity of electricity (b) spoken, e.g. the adventures of the migrating swallows! Physical actions help children to internalise scientific concepts.	*Valuable* in giving information about children's knowledge and understanding of scientific ideas.	No permanent record as evidence. Take photographs for Pupil Profiles.
Word mapping		
(a) word burrs (b) word lists (c) Venn diagrams (d) concept mapping	*Useful* in seeing the connections that children are making with their existing knowledge. Can sometimes provide evidence of understanding. Provides records which can be copied for the Pupil Profiles.	Requires pupils to have confidence in writing skills and vocabulary.
Concept cartoons		
Use concept cartoons for assessment, e.g. Figure 2.2 (Naylor and Keogh 2000)	*Valuable* in gaining information about children's scientific understanding and creative thinking. The level of conceptual understanding can be tailored to the individual or group.	Not easy to make a permanent record – use recall or tape recorder.
Presentations (as groups or individuals)		
Use one or several of the methods	*Useful* in giving information about about children's knowledge, understanding, ability to research and interpret this and communicate with others, and social skills.	No permanent record – use recalled notes or video record.

Pupil Profiles are excellent for discussions and for feedback to children, parents and colleagues. Positive feedback reinforces children's self-esteem and skills and encourages them to articulate their ideas. Able children respond well to specific praise, especially if it gives them room for negotiating or decision-making: 'I notice how much you helped Aftab with the dissolving. I know *you* knew what would happen. I have some other substances to dissolve and different

Last week, after dissolving the salt, I asked the children if we could get the salt back again.

Gina: If we stand it outside in the sun the water will dry up.

Selim: Yes – that thing . . . evaporate.

Today, five days later, we could see the salt crystals clinging to the sides and the string. We took some off and used the microscope for a closer look at the salt crystals.

Aaron: It's like ice!

Mary: It's a funny shape, like squares.

Jenny: It's like icebergs.

Albert: It's cuboids stuck together. They've grown up like steps.

Figure 1.1 Teacher's record at the end of a school day

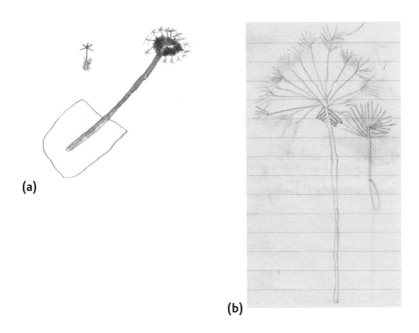

(a)

(b)

Figure 1.2 Dandelion 'clock' and single seed drawn by six-year-olds Lorna **(a)** and Jimmy **(b)**

solvents. Would you like to work on your own this time or bring Aftab with you?' All children respond positively to things going 'wrong' if there is a open-minded, scientific atmosphere where failure is just the start of another enquiry (e.g. a new problem to be solved), or part of the evaluating process. This takes the personal criticism out of evaluation and is less threatening. Children learn to criticise their own experiment and take it a step further by suggesting what they could do if they had more time. My research showed that given the opportunity, children as young as four years will evaluate their work critically and reflect on their own thinking processes, 'I don't know – I never thunk it before' (de Bóo 1999: 125).

Parents do not always find it easy to interpret children's work or responses at home and need the insight and enthusiasm of the teacher. Pupil Profiles focus

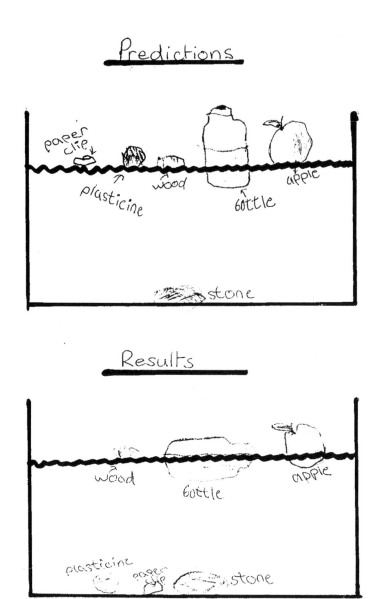

Figure 1.3 Predictions and results drawn by six-year-old Ale

their attention and allow the teacher to interpret children's achievements for them and make clear comparisons with national criteria.

Representative evidence of children's performance is ideal for discussions with colleagues in identifying scientifically able children and planning appropriate provision for them. Accumulated evidence helps us to develop school policies for the most able.

The Appendix gives Tables of Significant Attainment to aid identification of children's scientific abilities, knowledge and skills.

How to use this book

This book offers some strategies for teaching scientifically gifted children in the context of an ordinary classroom. In such a classroom we are often faced with

A. Richard (six years)

Reasons for not chopping down trees.

If we chop down trees, birds won't have any place to live and we'd have no fruit and no flowers and no contreeside (sic).

B. Krista (six years)

Once upon a time there was 20 little seed. It was the second day of spring. It was the time of the yare that the seeds get there names and one seed insted of listening, he chated to his frenind and so when all the other seeds had gone away, the tow seeds stad behind and said We have bine notty. Wot are our names? I will give you tow names. Roger is yos and cress, and yorus is Jimmy and buttercup. Now run a long now and plant yor selfs and they all lived happily ever after. The end.

C. Class question and answer book (five- to six-year-old children). Named children volunteer their own questions, different children write anonymous answers. Ayse (five years) wrote 'Why do bees have six legs?'

- *So they can walk.*
- *So they can go to the nectar.*
- *So they can stand up.*

Karis (six years) Why are bees black and orange?

- *Nice colour.*
- *Because it's their favourite colour.*
- *To attract the ladies.*

Figure 1.4 Examples of children's written work

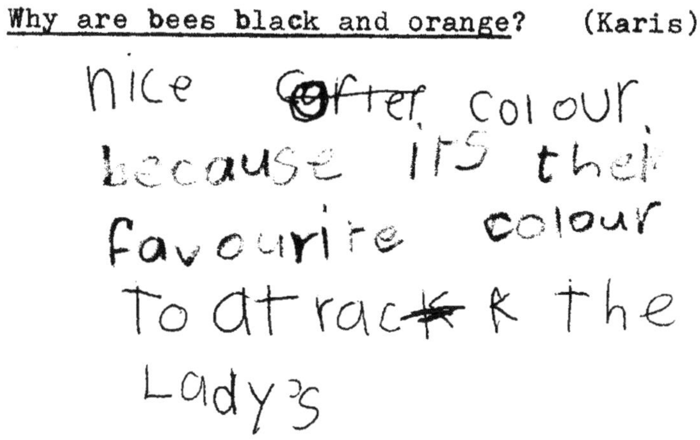

Figure 1.5 Karis's written answer to 'Why are bees black and orange?'

differentiating for a wide range of children, which can mean writing separate programmes for just one or two children in a class. The activities in this book have been written to give opportunities for all children to achieve something while giving scope for gifted children to learn more deeply and extensively.

Many of the activities will feel familiar – but it is not what you do but the way that you do it that produces exciting and successful results. Stimulating activities together with challenging questions encourage thinking skills and in-depth learning, and often prompt ideas for extended investigation by more able children.

Each activity is broken down as follows.

Introduction

The introduction explains the over-arching concept/s to the activity, gives background information and reminders about aspects of health and safety.

Activity

This describes appropriate starting points to the activity, resources needed, and how to develop the exploration or practical investigation to its conclusion. The resources may sometimes refer to the use of ICT, although specific programs are not cited as these would need to be compatible with individual school computers. However, the Useful Resources section at the end of the book gives some addresses and websites for useful software and research. Recommendations are made within each activity to ensure children's health and safety but it is always advisable to refer to the Association for Science Education (ASE) publication *Be Safe! Some Aspects of Safety in School Science and Technology for Key Stage 1 and 2* (ASE 2000).

Organisation

This suggests ways of working, whether friendship or ability groups or whole-class work, and provides details of children's concerns that need to be addressed. 'H&S' refers to health and safety procedures.

Questions to encourage thinking skills

These are usually open-ended, person-centred questions. They will encourage thinking skills and stimulate further scientific enquiries. The questions will also prompt responses that will provide evidence for assessment of children's skills, attitudes and knowledge.

Vocabulary

The words given here are the scientific terms that may be usefully brought into discussions with some or all children. When able children use these scientific terms, it can be revealing if we ask them to explain what *they* mean by the term.

Scientific/mathematical terms and units are also listed here. Younger and less able children from four to seven years may need to use non-standard units some or all of the time (handspans, cupfuls), but children begin to see the need for standard units when questioned about the 'fairness' of using non-standard units. Able children usually recognise this early on.

Extension and enrichment activities

It is not always appropriate to increase a child's quantity of knowledge in a linear way. It is better to develop the quality of learning or depth of knowledge and understanding. Extension and enrichment activities may be followed up by the whole class and/or by the most able children. They are intended to develop children's understanding of the principal concepts, expand the work across other areas of the curriculum, and encourage individual or group research. By including a range of ideas, many children will be able to participate on different occasions with these extension activities, thus reducing the perception of isolation or 'special treatment' for the more able children when they access extension work.

Points of significant attainment to look for

These outline the learning targets that may be achieved during the activity, identifying knowledge and understanding, scientific skills and attitudes. Not all children will achieve these targets but the list of statements gives an indication of what more able children may achieve.

Additional ideas and resources

This gives additional science or cross-curricular activities, relevant story or information books, poems and rhymes to recite and songs to sing. Full details of these books are provided in the Useful Resources section at the end of the book.

Appendix: Tables of Significant Attainment

National curricula (England, Wales, Scotland) have established much of the detail we might look for in all children's development in science. Based on these nationally agreed criteria, the Tables of Significant Attainment outline the development and progression of scientific skills, attitudes and knowledge. The concepts are set in the context of the activities in the book. Aspects of key vocabulary are listed. The details are based on the earlier book by Pat O'Brien (1998), *Teaching Scientifically Able Pupils in the Primary School* (to whom I give many thanks). For each table the list of learning outcomes is as defined in national curricula, showing the progression of skills, attitudes, and knowledge and understanding. This is designed to aid the identification of children's achievements for pupil profiling and reporting purposes.

Useful Resources

The Useful Resources section suggests some suitable resources to assist the practitioner, enrich the learning environment and encourage children's thinking and exploration.

Life Processes and Living Things

1. Me and myself
QCA links: 2A, 3A

Introduction

The principal concepts targeted in this section are (a) all humans belong to the same family but each individual is uniquely different, and (b) humans grow from babies through childhood to adults and then have babies of their own. These concepts are true regardless of country of origin, skin colour, height, weight, etc.

Activity

Starting point

Get help from a colleague to draw around your own silhouette, cut it out and pin it up before the children arrive. Introduce the silhouette as 'a new arrival in the class'. Discuss some of the missing features, such as hair (colour, length, straight/curly) and eyes (colour, shape).

On a subsequent day, produce a silhouette representing a baby and use for further discussion.

Development

Encourage the children to draw around each other's silhouette on white or pale coloured sugar paper and draw on as many external features as they can think of. Able children could add some internal organs onto their silhouette.

Discuss the similarities (eyes, arms, etc.) and any differences between the silhouettes. Compare eye colour and measure heights and use the data to make manual or ICT graphs such as the one shown in Figure 2.1 (see Useful Resources).

When using the baby silhouette, discuss the differences between babies and older children (heads, limbs, teeth, capabilities). Discuss what the children can do

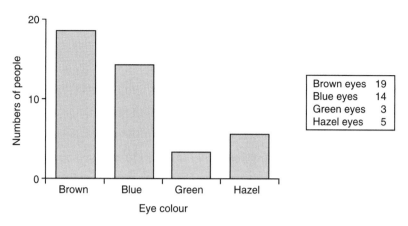

Figure 2.1 What colour are *your* eyes?

now but not when they were younger. Discuss growing and changes and what they will be able to do when they are older.

Conclusion

Label and mount the graph/s on one or two silhouettes with questions to invite interaction, such as 'How many children have brown eyes?'

Organisation

Work in ability groups of twos to draw around each silhouette and discuss the features. As and when able children complete one task, they can progress to another one. Pool all information in the plenary.

Questions to encourage thinking skills

- How can we tell if this belongs to a human being? How can you tell it isn't a horse? a rabbit? a bird? a fish?
- How are we the same as each other? Which features can be different?
- (with sensitivity) Are you like anyone else in your family?
- What can you do now that you couldn't do when you were babies? Why is that?
- What happens when we are old grannies and grandads? Will we be able to do everything then?
- When do you think we do our growing? How can we find out?
- What helps us to grow properly? Anything else?
- What would you like to do when you grow up – for a job? for excitement? for fun?

Vocabulary

animals, body, change, characteristics, compare, develop, different, ears, eyes, features, grow, human, inherit, organs, silhouette, similar

Extension and enrichment activities

- Make a list of family traditions and cultural traditions, such as visiting grandparents, celebrating birthdays and other festivals, eating special foods, etc. Use the information to make a poem about what is liked the most about family festivals.
- Make a chart of children's birthdays. Which months have most/least birthdays?
- Design a poster called 'Help old people'.
- Interview a granny or grandpa or old neighbour about what it was like when they were children. Make a presentation in a plenary discussion, inviting other children to add what they know from their experience.
- Discuss 'Shadow screen' No.12.2 in *Concept Cartoons in Science Education* by Stuart Naylor and Brenda Keogh (2000), as shown in Figure 2.2.

Figure 2.2 Shadow screen (Naylor and Keogh 2000)

Points of significant attainment to look for

Children:

- describe the differences between babies, children and older people
- know that human beings grow and change
- know that human beings vary from each other while still sharing many similarities
- co-operate with each other when collecting data on height and eye colour
- record data and use it to create and interpret simple charts and graphs
- think aloud in a speculative, hypothetical way by offering explanations for patterns
- know about external features of the human body (and internal organs as appropriate)
- show early understanding of the need for hygiene and care of ourselves
- show an awareness of consideration for other people.

Additional ideas and resources

- Collect photos of the children and of members of staff when babies or small children and mount for a 'Rogues Gallery' guessing game.

- Read: *Kipper Birthday* by Mick Inkpen. Picture Knights.

  Titch by Pat Hutchins. Red Fox Books.

  Tall Inside by Jean Richardson and Alice Englander. Picture Puffins.

  Me First by Helen Lesterand Lynn Munsinger. Macmillan.

  My Naughty Little Sister by Dorothy Edwards. Young Puffin.

- Recite: 'When I was one, I was just begun' in *Now We Are Six* by A. A. Milne.Methuen.

- Recite and use for pictures and collages: 'There was an old woman who lived in a shoe' (traditional rhyme).

2. Round my little finger
QCA link: 2C

Introduction

Our hands are one of the most sensitive parts of our bodies. We have hundreds of nerve endings in our fingertips sensing touch, temperature, pressure and pain. We receive and give information with our hands and the information can be pleasurable or unpleasant, caring or hostile, hazardous or even life-threatening: stroking a baby, touching a hot saucepan or fire. Young children have explored their environment from birth via their hands and their sensitive mouth. Now, they are developing sophisticated hand and eye co-ordinated motor skills. This makes studying the hands and sense of touch both fascinating and a good way of reinforcing the concept that 'all humans beings are alike and all individual humans are different'. We all have hands yet all our hands vary in size, shape, fingerprints, etc.

Activity

Starting point
Introduce the activity with a photocopy of your own hand. Show this and encourage as many questions as the children can think of about this and any other hands.

Development
If possible, make photocopies of the children's hands.

> **H&S:** Remind children to avoid looking at the light source during photocopying.

Additionally, have children draw around their own or each other's hands. Use the drawings and/or photocopies for the children to observe and compare characteristics of their hands. For example, compare the lengths of the thumbs with the little fingers – is there any difference? Measure the lengths of the middle fingers for class comparisons. Introduce the word and expression 'on average'.

Conclusion
Make a topic book on 'Our Hands' and include data and drawings.

Organisation

Children work in ability groups of twos or threes to draw their hands and offer questions, observations and measurements.

Questions to encourage thinking skills

- What do you notice about the hands? Anything else?
- What is the same? What differences can you see?
- Is your thumb longer than your little finger? What about other people?
- Which is the longest finger? How long is it?
- How many 'bendy parts'/knuckles do we have on our fingers? Why is that useful?
- What do we use our hands for? Anything else?
- What is the nicest thing you like to touch? What don't you like to touch?
- Can you think of something that you shouldn't ever touch?
- Can you think of any other animals that have two hands? two flippers? two wings?

Vocabulary

average, differences, fingers, fingerprints, forward, hand, hard, knuckles, larger, left, length, longer, palm, right, rough, same, shorter, silky, similarities, small, smooth, soft, squeezy, wide, width

Units: length: centimetres (cm)

Extension and enrichment activities

- Use a feely bag, initially with a few familiar objects. After the preliminary exploration, include objects that are either (a) unfamiliar or (b) similar to each other in either texture, size or shape so that descriptions must be precise.
- Compare the lengths of the middle fingers, record the data and make a chart by hand or using ICT (see Useful Resources).
- Provide children with a writing frame about our hands such as: 'I like to touch .... and ....; I do not like to touch .... or ....'. Able children could have additional sentences, such as: 'It is dangerous to touch .... and .... because ....'. Use the results to make a class book which can then be illustrated by the children.
- Play a guessing game by miming things we do with our hands – everyday things, jobs in the house or school, jobs done by people in the community.
- Design a poster to 'Wash your hands when you ....', perhaps explaining why.
- Collect different gloves and mittens, including rubber gloves, to make a labelled display or to create a classroom glove shop with prices in the role-play area.
- Make thick paint for dipping and printing hands. Cut out the prints and use to create pictures such as a tree, a peacock or a giant flower (see Figure 2.3).
- Use a commercial ink pad or DIY sponge pad and water-based ink to make children's fingerprints and compare these (e.g. whorls and arches).

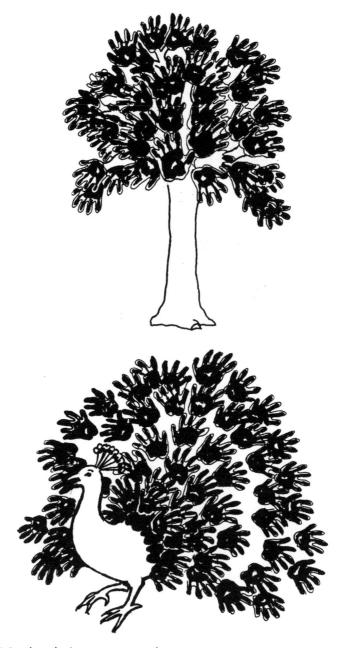

Figure 2.3 Using handprints to create pictures

Points of significant attainment to look for

Children:

- observe and describe to others the features of the hands

- ask questions and use first-hand experience to seek answers

- use simple equipment effectively to measure length of fingers

- record their data and create a simple bar graph/bar chart (manually or by ICT)

- show evidence of thinking out loud, speculating

- show emerging knowledge of what an 'average' is

- show knowledge of the variation in human hands while knowing that hands are similar
- show some understanding of health and safety and hygiene.

Additional ideas and resources

- Persuade children or parents who know traditional dances involving their hands to demonstrate their art. Use this as a stimulus for a creative movement lesson.
- Read: *Feel!* by Morris, N. and Stevenson, P. Firefly Books.
- Play: 'Tom Thumb, Tom Thumb, where are you?' in *Action Rhymes and Games* by Max de Bóo. Scholastic.
- Sing: 'Heads and shoulders, knees and toes' in *Okki Tokki Unga* edited by B. Harrop. A & C Black.

    'One finger, one thumb, keep moving' in *Action Rhymes and Games* by Max de Bóo. Scholastic.

---

3.   Best foot forward!
QCA link: 2A

Introduction

Whether studying the feet or faces or height, the concept to be learned is the same: all human beings belong to the same species and yet each individual human being is unique. Our feet share characteristics with many other animals: we have five toes (like fingers) as do monkeys, orang-utans, rats and bats. Even the prehistoric horse had five toes before evolving over time into walking on its middle fingernails (hooves). Our feet have evolved too – into giving us a flexible base on which to balance upright, walk, jump and run. Feet are an appropriate study for younger children, accessible without causing offence (usually), and it is important to be aware of good foot care and hygiene early on.

Activity

Starting point

Before investigating the feet, arrange a visit to a local shoe shop and see how the assistants measure the feet. Whether a visit is possible or not, encourage the children to ask as many questions as possible in advance about 'Feet and Footware'. Record their questions on a flipchart or the whiteboard for all to see.

Development

In the classroom, draw around each foot on paper either bare or wearing socks and cut these out. (NB: It is not always possible to be accurate in such drawings. If children are anxious, do them again. The scientific purpose is satisfied by comparing and measuring different things.)

Discuss the similarities and differences between the left and right feet. Measure and compare children's foot lengths and compare with shoe sizes. Draw around the shoes and cut out. Overlay the cut-out feet on the cut-out shoes and compare. (NB: This doesn't always reveal what we expect – bare feet may spread out more than inside a shoe!)

More able children could draw around the feet on squared paper to compare the area of each foot.

Conclusion

Create a classroom shoe shop in the creative-play area, with tape measures and assorted shoes and slippers.

Organisation

Work in ability groups of twos to draw around each other's feet and shoes. As and when able children complete one task, they can progress to another one, e.g. comparing the area of each foot. Pool all information in the plenary.

Questions to encourage thinking skills

- What do notice about all our feet? What is the same? What is different?
- How many toes do we have? Is that the same for everyone?
- Which shoe size/s do most of us take?
- Do you think that tall children have the biggest shoe size? Do short children take the smallest size? How can we find out?
- How many parts of our feet can bend?
- How many different things can we do with our feet?
- Why do you think we have nails on our toes and fingers?
- How can we keep our feet healthy?

Vocabulary

area, care, cleanliness, exercise, healthy, hygiene, length, scattergraph, size, trend, width

Units: height: metres (m) centimetres (cm)   area: square cm (sq cm/cm^2)

Extension and enrichment activities

- Children make observational drawings of their own feet from above and/or someone else's foot from the side.
- Make a class book about feet with children's questions (written by them or an adult) leaving space for other children to suggest the answers.
- Make a class graph about shoe sizes and encourage children to interpret the data.

- Dramatise the story of 'The Elves and the Shoemaker' from the point of view of the elves. Add a musical accompaniment and show the drama in Sharing Assembly.
- Play counting games in 5s, e.g. 1, 2, 3, 4, clap, 6, 7, 8, 9, clap. Try with every second (third, fourth) number silent and replaced with a clap. (Mistakes are usually a source of laughter!)

Points of significant attainment to look for

Children:

- describe what they notice/observe about feet
- ask questions and use first-hand experience to seek answers to these
- help to plan and carry out investigations on height and shoe size
- record measurements and use the data to see comparisons and patterns
- create and interpret simple charts and graphs
- offer explanations for patterns based on first-hand experience and prior knowledge
- know that human beings vary from each other while still sharing many similarities
- know about feet and toes as external features of the human body
- show early understanding of the need for hygiene and care of our feet.

Additional ideas and resources

- In PE, create simple repetitive dance movements or practise traditional movement rhymes such as 'Ring a ring o' roses' and 'In and out the dusty bluebells'.
- Read: *The Elves and the Shoemaker* (traditional). Ladybird Easy Reading Books.
- Recite: '1, 2, 3, 4, 5, once I caught a fish alive' (traditional rhyme).
            'Timothy Tim' in *Now We Are Six* by A. A. Milne. Methuen.
- Sing: 'Five little speckled frogs' in *Appusskidu* edited by B. Harrop. A & C Black.
            'Ten green bottles' (traditional song).

---

4.   Two tall trees
QCA link: 2C

Introduction

Trees are the 'lungs of the Earth'. They produce more atmospheric oxygen for us to breathe than any other green plants other than ocean algae (phytoplankton).

Recognising and investigating natural phenomena is good science. Preserving and protecting trees is good for our survival as well as good citizenship.

Activity

Starting point

Choose some local trees (street, park or woodland), preferably native species. Collect identification materials from books and websites (see Useful Resources) and get permission for field visits if required.

> **H&S:** Remind children that we must not eat the fruit from some trees for safety's sake: hazelnuts, yes, but horse chestnuts (conkers), no. Some children have allergies to nuts.

Development

Explore the trees with the senses: look, feel, smell (caution with hay fever sufferers) and listen (rustling leaves? birds in the canopy?). Draw or photograph the trees.

Do bark rubbings with paper and crayons. Depending on the season, collect a few leaves, twigs, flowers, fruit (e.g. conkers, sycamore seeds, acorns). Draw these in the field or in the classroom.

Encourage the children to suggest ways in which they could find out or estimate the girth or circumference, height and age of the trees without climbing up or cutting the trees down.

- To compare tree girths – Use string to measure the girth of the different trees at shoulder height. Knot the strings into circles and mount on card to record the comparison of the trees' girths as shown in Figure 2.4.

- To work out the approximate age of a tree – Measure the girth in centimetres with tape measures and use mental arithmetic or calculators to obtain the approximate age of the tree by dividing the tree girth's circumference by 2.5 (tree standing alone), or by 2 (avenue of trees) or by 1.5 (dense woodland). Use this data to make bar charts comparing the ages of the trees (i.e. 36 cm ÷ 2 = 18 years). See Figure 2.5.

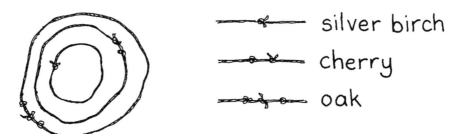

Figure 2.4 Comparing tree girths

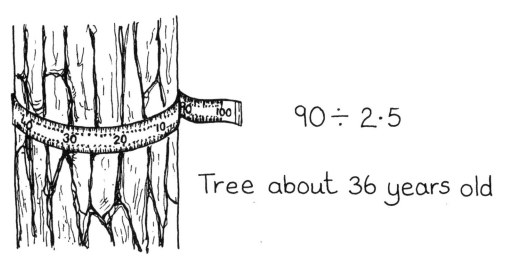

90 ÷ 2·5

Tree about 36 years old

Figure 2.5 Estimating the age of a tree by measuring its girth

- To estimate the height of the trees there are two methods –
    1. Stand a child beside a tree and use eye and fingers to count the number of 'child heights' of the tree (Figure 2.6).
    2. Walk away from the tree to a distance where, by bending down and looking through your legs, you can just see the top of the tree (Figure 2.7). The distance from the tree is approximately equal to the height of the tree (roughly an isosceles triangle).

    Accept differences of opinion in all cases and agree an overall average height.

Height of a tree = 4 times Amy

Figure 2.6 Estimating the height of a tree by using 'child heights'

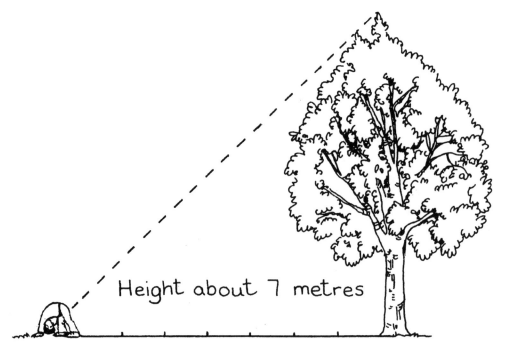

Height about 7 metres

Figure 2.7 Estimating the height of a tree by the 'isosceles triangle method'

Use some of the collected leaves to make crayon rubbings and/or plaster casts of the leaves. Identify the trees by using secondary sources, i.e. books and websites (see Useful Resources).

Conclusion

Record and illustrate all results in a class topic book or group books.

Organisation

Work in ability groups of four with each group 'adopting' a tree of their own. The outcomes are dependent on the group, with more able children expected to make more accurate measurements, explain conditions and do further research. Groups can take responsibility for displays – either a single display modified every two to three days or group displays.

Questions to encourage thinking skills

- Why do you think the trees grow here? What is a good place for trees to grow? Why do you think that?
- Are any of the trees the same as each other? Are any of them different? How?
- I wonder why trees are different from each other? Any other reasons?
- Why are trees important for animals, such as insects or birds?
- What might happen to a tree if the weather gets too hot and dry?
- Do you know what usually happens to a tree if the bark is stripped off? (It dies – growth takes place just under the bark. Some trees can survive by losing some bark, e.g. London plane, the eucalyptus.)
- How many different ways can we use trees?

Vocabulary

adopt, autumn, average, bark, breathe, canopy, change, compare, conditions, differences, distance, environment, estimate, flower, fruit, girth, grow, height, identify, leaf, light, measure, nuts, oxygen, produce, protect, roots, season, seeds, similarities, spring, summer, survive, tree, trunk, winter

Units: length: centimetres (cm) metres (m)

Extension and enrichment activities

- Use books, ICT, parents, to:
  - find out about trees such as the giant redwood, monkey puzzle, tulip tree, bonsai, palo boracho ('drunken stick') tree, Turkey oak, Chinese windmill-palm, strawberry tree.
  - create a set of questions for other children, teachers, parents for a weekly quiz and/or a class question book for display and for anyone to add their suggested answers.
- Debate the arguments for cutting and keeping trees: 'We shouldn't cut down the trees!'
- Use poster tubes, card and tissue or crêpe paper to create a miniature woodland in a part of the classroom or corridor. Challenge the children to make the trees stable, upright and safe without roots.
- Join the Woodland Trust and become a 'Nature Detective' (www.phenology.org.uk and www.woodland-trust.org.uk) recording seasonal changes online and contribute to data collection on climate change.

Points of significant attainment to look for

Children:

- know about and describe the features of living trees such as roots, trunk and leaves
- make suggestions about how to find things out and collect data to answer questions
- know how to use simple equipment safely and effectively to estimate and measure quantities
- use secondary sources, including ICT (texts, websites, etc.) to find information
- record information using graphs and ICT where appropriate and communicate the conclusions
- think aloud in debates, showing consideration for living things
- use knowledge of living things to describe conditions needed for trees to survive
- know why trees are suited to a particular environment
- know that trees are a benefit to living things and suggest ways of protecting them.

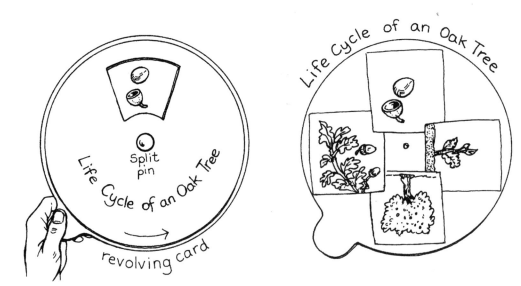

Figure 2.8 Making a revolving tree cycle card

Additional ideas and resources

- Photocopy and reduce the the children's drawings or use photographs or images from websites or other sources. Stick onto card as shown in Figure 2.8 to make revolving tree cycle cards, either from the seed to the full grown tree or the seasonal cycle of spring through to winter.

- Read: *The Tree* by Tim Vyner. Collins Picture Lions.

- Recite: 'I had a little nut tree' (traditional nursery rhyme)

            'Underneath the spreading chestnut tree' in *Action Rhymes and Games* by Max de Bóo. Scholastic.

            'Before tea' in *When We Were Very Young* by A. A. Milne. Methven.

- Sing: 'The tree in the wood' in *Sing a Song One* edited by Bird *et al.* Nelson.

---

5.   Beans means growth!
QCA links: 1B, 2C, 3B

Introduction

Germination of seeds usually takes place in the dark but once germinated, plants need light on their leaves to grow (photosynthesis). Conditions for growth include moisture and air (for photosynthesis) and a temperature suitable for that particular plant. Some plants have evolved to survive hot and dry conditions by growing thickened leaves and stems (e.g. cactus) or cold, windy and dry conditions by having thin needle-like leaves (e.g. pine trees). In the temperate climate of the UK, native plants have evolved to respond to moderate rainfall, temperature and sunlight. Climate change is now affecting the environment – native plants and animals in the ecosystem, including ourselves.

Activity

Starting point

Prepare for the activity by sowing six pots with four or five broad beans in each, in non-peat compost about two to three weeks in advance (beans are usually easy to grow).

Development

Show the children the growing bean plants. From two of the pots extract a few of the bean shoots carefully for each group of children to have one each for careful observation, labelling and drawing (see Figure 2.9). Use the remaining four pots of the sprouting beans for investigating how they will grow under the following conditions

1. in the light with regular watering
2. in the dark with regular watering
3. in the light without water
4. in the dark without water.

Invite the children to predict which plant will grow 'best' – and what they mean by 'best'. (Try to ensure that the temperature is more-or-less the same for each of these sets of conditions as including another variable such as temperature can be too confusing for most children.)

Observe and measure the plants over a week or two and discuss the results.

Conclusion

Draw or write an account of what was done and what happened.

Organisation

With enough bean shoots, this can be carried out with a whole class involved in the observation and drawing, followed by all involved in watching while the

Figure 2.9 A sprouting bean

growing pots are set up for the investigation. Children can be invited to recommend suitable locations for light and dark and a rota of responsibility for the watering on a daily basis.

Questions to encourage thinking skills

- What do you notice about these plants?
- How long have the roots grown in two weeks? How tall have the stems grown in two weeks?
- What do you think the plants need to make them grow? How can we find out?
- What do you think will happen to the plants in the dark? the ones that have no water?
- Why do you think that will happen?

Vocabulary

absorb, grow, leaf, leaves, moisture, roots, seeds, shoots, sprout, stem, temperature

Units: centimetres (cm)

Extension and enrichment activities

- Discuss 'Seeds in the dark' No. 6.1 in *Concept Cartoons in Science Education* by Stuart Naylor and Brenda Keogh (2000) as shown in Figure 2.10.
- Place some broad beans between the sides of glass jars and an internal collar of blotting paper. Rinse with water daily. Discuss how seeds might grow without soil. Transplant into pots with soil when roots and shoots have developed and repot as the plants get bigger until, weather permitting, the plants can be planted outdoors with stakes.
- More able children could make a selection of leaves and use to explain to everyone what a leaf is for/can do.
- Debate what might happen to our local plants and animals if the weather changed to hot and dry all year round.
- Write a story beginning 'Once upon a time, the weather got so hot that all the plants began to die. So . . .'

Points of significant attainment to look for

Children:

- seek answers to questions
- make predictions
- help to plan and carry out investigations
- make observations and record measurements
- interpret data and offer explanations for the results

Figure 2.10 Seeds in the dark (Naylor and Keogh 2000)

- communicate findings to others, using scientific terminology
- know that plants need light and water to grow
- recognise and identify different parts of plants (leaf, stem, root, etc.)
- know that seeds grow into flowering plants
- are aware of some of the effects of changing conditions such as temperature and rainfall on the local habitat.

Additional ideas and resources

● Grow mustard and cress seeds on blotting paper or on cotton wool inside half egg shells. Use felt-tip pens to paint faces on the shells – the green cress is the 'hair'.

- Read: *Jack and the Beanstalk.* Picture Puffin.

  The Little Red Hen and the Grains of Wheat. Ladybird Easy Reading Books.

  Out and About by Shirley Hughes. Walker Books.

- Sing: 'Katie's garden' in *Appusskidu* edited by B. Harrop. A & C Black.

  'Little seed' in *Sing a Song One* edited by B. Harrop. Nelson.

6. Fruit and veg
QCA links: 1B, 2B

Introduction

Edible plants are fundamentally important to our survival. They contain carbohydrates, vitamins and minerals, and fibre for roughage. Recent health advice suggests we should eat 'five-a-day', especially a 'rainbow' of fruit and veg: the colours are an indication of the vitamins and minerals, e.g. tomatoes (red), carrots (orange), broccoli (green), blackberries (blue/purple), leeks (white). Fruit and vegetables can also help children to identify parts of plants.

> **H&S:** Check with parents about children's food allergies and always avoid using peanuts. Remind children not to eat things without an adult's permission.

Activity

Starting point

Arrange to visit and/or carry out a preliminary visit to a supermarket or local greengrocer to identify some of the foods to observe and eat. Buy items that reflect different edible parts of a plant: roots (carrots, parsnips, radishes), tubers (potatoes, sweet potatoes, ginger), leaves (lettuce, cabbage), stems (spring onions, celery, asparagus), flowers (broccoli, cauliflower), seeds (peas, green beans), fruit (apples, cucumber, tomatoes, bananas, blackberries).

> **H&S:** Choose nuts with care and with reference to children's allergies.

Development

Explore the fruits and vegetables using the senses and handlenses. More able children could also measure and weigh the fruits and vegetables with standard units. Sort the items by colour, size, etc. Discuss whereabouts on the plant the different foods grow. Choose a fruit or veg to draw and/or predict whereabouts on the plant it would grow. Discuss the roles of the parts of the plant in the living processes of the plant – storing food for growth, developing seeds for new plants, etc.

Conclusion

Display the drawings and predictions with labels and questions.

Organisation

With an outside visit, the children will be grouped in numbers according to the available adults. Supporting adults can be given a list of useful questions to ask (such as those listed below). In the classroom, if there are enough fruits and vegetables, the activity can be carried out as a whole class with children in pairs, sharing a fruit and a vegetable for drawing or discussing their predictions. Pool ideas in the plenary discussion.

Questions to encourage thinking skills

- What do you notice about the fruit and vegetables?
- Where do you think they come from? And before that?
- Whereabouts on the plant do you think it grows? Draw your predictions.
- Which do you think is heavier – potatoes or apples? How can we find out?
- How do we store the foods to keep them fresh and stop them decaying too quickly? Is there any other way?
- What could happen if we ate food that wasn't fresh or wasn't cooked properly?
- Where do you think popcorn and cornflakes come from? What about crisps and shreddies?

Vocabulary

bulb, cooked, decay, flower, fresh, grow, healthy, leaf, leaves, petals, plant, raw, seed, stem, tuber

Units: weight: grams (g)

Extension and enrichment activities

- Take a potted herb (e.g. parsley or mint), remove from the pot and compare the parts of this plant with some of the fruit and veg before repotting.
- Cut open the fruits and vegetables and explore the insides. Use some of the vegetables to make crudités with a dip made by mixing equal quantities of tomato ketchup with salad cream. Use some of the fruit to make a fresh fruit salad.

- Design a poster urging everyone to 'Eat more fruit and vegetables', and why.

- Find the country of origin of some of the items using information on the package, the shop labels and a map or globe.

- Make a poem in the form of a shopping list for food, e.g. 'A kilo of pears, a bunch of bananas, some ripe red apples, . . .'.

- Use ICT (word processing, clip art, e.g. Sherston Software 'Clip Art' or Research Machines 'Easiteach Science') to write out and decorate a recipe on 'How to make fruit salad'.

Points of significant attainment to look for

Children:

- explore fruit and vegetables using the senses

- record observations by drawing

- estimate and measure weights

- sort and classify by size, shape, etc.

- carry out fair tests on growing plants

- describe and identify different parts of plants (stem, root, etc.)

- offer reasonable hypotheses/explanations about unfamiliar parts of plant

- know that seeds grow into plants

- are aware of the need for a healthy diet

- know that foods can decay.

Additional ideas and resources

- Draw and cut out labelled and numbered parts of a flowering plant (e.g. sunflower with one stem, two leaves, four roots, eight petals, eight seeds) to make either a jigsaw or four sets for a dice game: roots = 1, stem = 2, leaves = 3 each, petals = 4 each, seeds = 5 each, any part = 6 + extra turn.

- Read: *I Will Not Ever NEVER Eat a Tomato* by Lauren Child. Orchard Books.

    Green Eggs and Ham by Dr Seuss. Beginner Books.

- Recite: 'Rice pudding' in *When We Were Very Young* by A. A. Milne. Methuen.

    'Peter Piper picked a peck of pickled pepper' (traditional tongue twister).

- Sing: 'Hungry, hungry, I am hungry' in *Apusskidu* edited by B. Harrop. A & C Black.

7. Big bean and Susie sunflower
QCA link: 1B

Introduction

The focus of this activity is variation and classification of living things. Classification is not only an important scientific skill, it is a life skill whereby we make sense of our world by organising things and events. Classifying allows us to adopt effective strategies to deal with similar things – whether 'toxic plants' or 'jobs requiring a professional plumber'. Children are often given too little opportunity to practise this skill. In the activities below, children are encouraged to use a range of methods to sort and classify and offer acceptable explanations for their chosen criteria. Depending on their age and ability, children's initial choices will include personal and subjective criteria from their point of view (e.g. 'the cuddly toy likes jam'), as well as descriptive choices (same colour, shape) or higher order grouping (alive, not alive).

Activity

Starting point
Make two collections, A and B.

Collection A: Collect about 12 to 15 different objects, living and non-living and a few which are no longer alive but originally came from a living thing (e.g. fruit or wood). Select some that are familiar to the children (e.g. cuddly toy, wooden brick, flower, seed, small pot plant, candle, apple, shell, rock, piece of bread, a real woolly hat, a glue stick, a small jar of jam) and a few that are less familiar (e.g. sweet potato or coconut, a squash ball, an ocarina, a stone or an amethyst). A large general selection allows us to offer a different choice of objects to each group of children to sort (see Figure 2.11), resulting in interest and innovative responses.

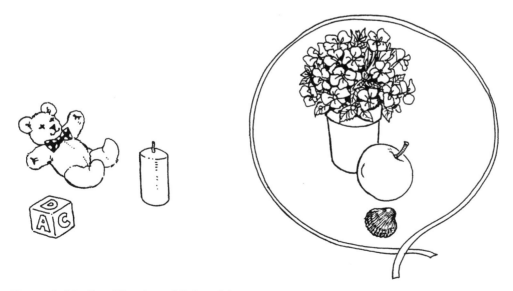

Figure 2.11 Classification of living things

Collection B: Collect a group of seeds, bulbs and tubers (e.g. runner beans, orange pips, seeds of sunflower, cress, nasturtium, carrot, tomato, apple and onions, hyacinth or other flowering bulb, potatoes, coconut, avocado, mango or passion fruit seeds).

> **H&S:** Remind children that not all seeds are edible and it is important to wash hands after handling seeds (some seeds are coated with chemicals to hasten growth or resist bacterial infection).

Development

With each collection, show a mixed group of objects (five to six objects for younger children, seven to eight for older children). Children sort the objects, choosing which ones 'belong together' and explain their choices. Approve their choices then regroup the objects and repeat, asking for different criteria for 'belonging together'. Repeat two or three times.

Produce one or more 'new' objects and encourage discussion as to which set these will belong to and why. This allows children to confirm their classification and challenges their thinking skills. The children might think of other objects that might belong to the sets. Sorting like this combined with requests for explanations encourages *all* children to think and allows able children to reveal their existing knowledge.

At some point in the sorting, it is useful for the adult to 'have his or her turn' and select by criteria such as (A) Living/Non-living and (B) Seeds, Bulbs, Tubers/Others, together with the question 'Can you guess why I have sorted them like this?'. Depending on the ability of the children, they may know, but did not choose that reason for sorting. With (A), it may be sufficient to explain that 'these things grow'/'these don't', while more able children can discuss the part of the plant from which they came and how they grow.

Conclusion

Use Venn hoops to make a changing display of the sets. Children could draw the sets of their own choice.

Organisation

Use groups of four to five children, either social or ability groups. Differentiation is effected by offering a range of open-ended, person-centred questions. Able children will offer more knowledgeable responses and more creative explanations (whether right or wrong scientifically). Approve all choices and explanations for phenomena, including subjective or less experienced responses – even talented children feel more secure in their apparently 'uncommon' (higher order thinking) choices when they see that personal and other choices are all accepted positively.

Questions to encourage thinking skills

- Which objects belong together? Why do you think that?
- Can you think of different ways in which these things belong together? Why do you think that? Where would this one belong?
- What does this one/these remind you of?
- Why do you think I have put these objects together?
- What is different about all the seeds? What is the same/similar about all these seeds?
- Do you think all the bean/sunflower/etc. seeds are the same size, shape, weight? (NB: When weighing small seeds, try weighing by 10s or 20s or in a small container.)
- Will all the bean seeds grow into beans? Could they grow into sunflowers? Why do you think that?
- Whereabouts on the plant do you think the seeds might develop?

Vocabulary

bulb, different, flower, fruit, germinate, group, grow, living, never alive, non-living, object, parent plant, predict, produce, reason, reproduce, roots, same, seed, shoots, similar, tuber, weigh

Non-standard units (e.g. counters) and standard units of weight: grams (g)

Extension and enrichment activities

- Grow groups of the same seeds. Look at different conditions for growth and ask the children to predict which ones will grow best where (see Activity 5, Beans means growth!).
- Bring in unknown fruits and encourage children to *draw* their predictions of where the seeds are found in or on these fruits: e.g. kiwi, mango, passion fruit, bananas and strawberries (we tend to ignore the seeds in or on these). Then cut open and discuss and/or draw.
- Invite parents to give fruit recipes or come into the classroom to cook with the children.
- Offer differentiated tasks: (a) Draw a sequence of pictures illustrating 'How to grow a seed' or (b) Write a story 'Once upon a time, Greeny the Grass seed wanted to grow as big as his friends, Big Bean and Susie Sunflower. So . . .'
- Debate the advantages of having artificial flowers and grass or real grass and flowers.

Points of significant attainment to look for

Children:

- observe objects closely and describe their features using eyes and magnifiers

– use equipment like handlenses and microscopes safely and effectively

– sort objects into groups, according to observable similarities and differences

– explain the criteria for their choices (texture, use, origin, properties)

– know about parts of plants such as seeds, leaves, etc.

– know that living things grow and that seeds, bulbs and tubers/roots can all grow into new plants (NB: Some seeds won't germinate and grow into plants but this concept is inappropriate for most children at this age.)

– describe some of the differences between living and non-living things.

Additional ideas and resources

- Use a range of seeds and glue to make pictures and patterns.
- Read: *The Secret Garden* by Frances Hodgson Burnett. Puffin.
- Recite: 'Mary, Mary, quite contrary' (traditional rhyme).
- Sing: 'The flowers that grow in the garden' in *Someone's Singing, Lord*. A & C Black.

  'One potato, two potato' in *Apusskidu* edited by B. Harrop. A & C Black.

8. Fish without fingers
QCA link: 2C

Introduction

Although it may not be possible to study fish in their own environment (unless you have goldfish or a nearby pond), fish represent a wonderful example of animals that are uniquely adapted to their environment. Fish extract dissolved oxygen from the water by breathing through gills, they have body shapes adapted to living in water (canoe or submarine shape or flat fish), overlapping scales for streamlined swimming, and flexible skeletons. Fish are often adapted or camouflaged by having paler underbellies (less easily seen from underneath against the light surface) and darker on top (harder to see against the darker sea depths). Finally, it is valuable for children to experience fish as living things rather than simply associate them with small cuboid fish fingers!

Activity

Starting point

If possible, arrange a visit to a local fishmonger or fish stall in the supermarket. If this is not feasible, bring in some fresh fish to study at first hand and invite as many questions as possible about fish. Look at more than one type of fish, e.g. a whole trout, fresh sardines and a whole plaice or sole. Ask the fishmonger to gut the fish and give you the skeleton with the head attached.

> **H&S:** Fresh fish will not keep easily after being 'explored' in the classroom – cook that day or dispose of safely. Remind children to wash their hands thoroughly before and after touching the fish.

Development

In the shop and later in the classroom, encourage the children to use their eyes only to begin with, then the other senses to observe, describe and explain the characteristics of the fish, head and skeleton. Expand the fins to show the area of water they can push on and in which direction when they are swimming. Use handlenses and microscopes to look closely at the scales.

Conclusion

Display information and story books about fish, children's poems and drawings and models.

Organisation

For a visit to the fishmonger or supermarket, you would need additional adult support and this would be ideal in the classroom too. That way, all children would be involved in the initial exploration without having to wait. Children could sit in larger friendship groups of five or six, rotating objects to observe closely: e.g. Group 1: skeleton A, Group 2: filleted fish A, Group 3: skeleton B, Group 4: filleted fish B, Group 5: smaller fish. After five minutes, the fish are swapped from table to table. Support adults could be given a list of the questions below to challenge children's thinking.

If no support adults are available, use rotating friendship groups of four or five children, looking closely at one or two items only. Share all the ideas in the joint plenary.

Questions to encourage thinking skills

- What do you notice about the fish? Anything else?
- How many eyes do the fish have? Where are they? Why is that, do you think?
- What colour are the fish? Are they the same colour all over? Can you think of any reasons for that?
- What do you notice about the fish skeleton? Is it heavy? How does it move?
- Fish need oxygen to breathe just like us. We get ours from the air. Can you guess how the fish get their oxygen from the water?
- Can we breathe underwater? Unaided? Do you think fish can breathe out of water?
- Do you think that fish swim like us? Why do you think some swimmers use flippers?
- How many of us like to eat fish? What about fish fingers?
- What do you think little fish feed on? What do big fish feed on?

Vocabulary

adapted, air, breathe, colour, environment, eyes, fins, flexible, gills, habitat, oxygen, scales, shoal, skeleton, skin, streamlined, tail, teeth, underbelly

Extension and enrichment activities

- Make an impression of the fish skeleton in modelling clay or use the actual skeleton to make a plaster cast (the same day!) with plaster of Paris.

> **H&S:** Dispose of the remains of the fish hygienically and safely. Use the plaster cast for continuing discussion.

- Use books, websites, etc. to research information about interesting fish and other animals living in the sea: angel fish, flying fish, whales and dolphins, sea urchins, sharks, crabs. Use prints, drawings or photocopies of these to create a class book on 'Sea Animals' with space for children to add further information.
- Dramatise a story: The fishermen chase the fish, the fish are caught, turned into fish fingers, sold in the supermarket, then eaten by children! Accompany the story with music.
- Write a story beginning: 'I am a little shark. Nobody liked me and I had no friends so one day I . . .!'

Points of significant attainment

Children:

- use their senses to explore and describe their observations about fish
- describe some of the characteristics that make fish suited to their environment
- know some of the characteristics of living animals (move, breathe, feed, respond to stimuli)
- know features shared by fish and humans beings (eyes, mouths, skeletons)
- think aloud and speculate what might happen if fish and other water animals are removed from their habitat
- begin to be aware of the relationship between predator and prey
- use secondary sources, including ICT, to find relevant information about fish around the world
- generate a graph manually or using ICT and interpret the graph to others.

Additional ideas and resources

- Make a graph of fish eaters/fish finger eaters/non-fish eaters and interpret the results.

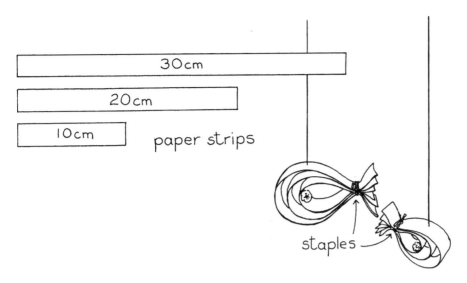

Figure 2.12 How to make a fish mobile

- Make a fish mobile. For each child, cut out three strips of paper, 2 cm wide by 10 cm, 20 cm and 30 cm. Colour in each side of the strips, then staple the ends together in ascending order to form the tail (see Figure 2.12). Add an eye with a twist of coloured tissue paper stuck on the inside length. Suspend on cotton thread from coat hangers or similar.

- Read: *What is a Fish?* by Robert Snedden and Oxford Scientific Films. Belitha Press.

    One Fish, Two Fish, Red Fish, Blue Fish by Dr Seuss. Beginner Books.

- Recite: 'A little fish' in *Sing a Song One* edited by Bird *et al.* Nelson.

- Sing: 'Fishing' in *Okki Tokki Unga* edited by B. Harrop. A & C Black.

    '1, 2, 3, 4, 5, once I caught a fish alive' (traditional song).

9.   Our six-legged friends
QCA links: 1A, 3A

Introduction

Children may not think of insects and other small creatures as being animals so this is a concept to target. The other principal concept targeted here is that animals and plants are adapted to their environment. However important human beings seem to be, we could not survive without very small creatures in our environment: insects pollinate flowering plants that produce food, worms and beetles break down organic waste into soil, birds control the numbers of insects and beetles. Living things we cannot see contribute to our well-being – the bacteria in our gut help us to digest our food and even fight more harmful bacteria.

Even squeamish children can become excited when they get the opportunity to see and identify small creatures. Studying small animals is best carried out from late spring to autumn and will involve at least one outdoor visit with the children.

> **H&S:** Remind children of the need to wash their hands before and after handling animals and plants.

Activity

Starting point

Arrange a visit to an area with ground plants and/or deciduous bushes and low trees. Avoid evergreen trees and bushes because these support fewer varieties of organism. Prepare DIY and commercial equipment (available from TTS Group Ltd, see Useful Resources) to catch and temporarily store small creatures safely:

- pooters (to suck up creatures safely and transfer to an observation jar) – see Figure 2.13a
- plastic bags (for transporting leaf litter)
- observation jars (transparent plastic containers – some of which have lenses in the lids)
- a shake sheet (shake a low branch over this and transfer creatures using a pooter) – see Figure 2.13b
- sweep net (sweep through a bush, branches or ground plants)
- small trowel or shovel (for scooping up leaf litter or soil)

It might be useful to catch and keep a few snails or woodlice *in advance* so as to ensure some animals are available to observe. It is possible to keep them for a few more days if you create an appropriate indoor habitat (see Figure 2.14). Use a water tank or similar container with an aerated cover. At one end, place a piece of damp cloth (keep damp) and place a few pebbles and a piece of wood inside to create a dark, damp area (essential for woodlice). Supply fresh lettuce leaves daily.

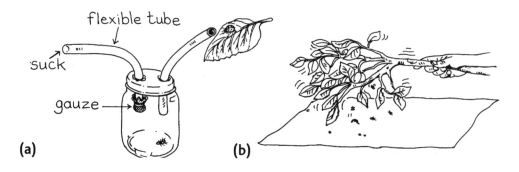

(a) **(b)**

Figure 2.13 (a) Pooter and **(b)** shake sheet to catch insects and other small creatures

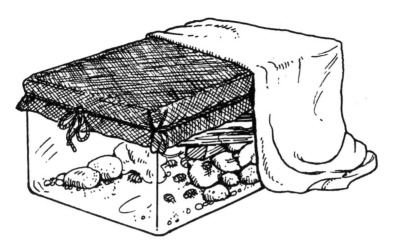

Figure 2.14 An indoor habitat for woodlice

Development

> **H&S:** Remind children to tread carefully near plants and small animals.

Use the equipment to collect some animals to take indoors for observation. In the classroom, use eyes, handlenses and microscopes to observe the animals closely. Note sizes, colours, legs and any patterns of movement within their habitat. Discuss possible reasons for this.

Choose an animal to draw and/or photograph, and use books and CD-ROMs such as Anglia Multimedia 'Garden Life' to identify some of the creatures. Dorling Kindersley's *Encyclopedia of Nature* or *Seashore Life* and *Garden Life* (Anglia Multimedia) are good resources. Release the animals into their original habitat as soon as possible.

Conclusion

Design and display posters reminding everyone to take care of plants and animals.

Organisation

If the outdoor location is nearby, there may be no need for auxiliary support. The children can be grouped in ability groups of threes with the instruction to stay together. They would work indoors in the same groups.

Questions to encourage thinking skills

- What do you notice about the animals?
- Was it easy to find them? Why/why not?
- What colour are they? What colours are best for hiding among leaves? in the soil? on flowers?

- How many legs do they have? How do they move?
- Where do they like to live? Why is that, do you think?
- What do you think the snails like to eat? How can we find out?
- How are the animals the same as us? How are they different?

Vocabulary

alive, animal, camouflage, care, conditions, dead, food, grow, habitat, healthy, hide, predator, prey, snail, survive, woodlouse, woodlice

Extension and enrichment activities

- Use books and CD-ROMs to identify some of the creatures. More able children could create a key for the whole class using questions with yes/no answers to sort the animals successively, for example:

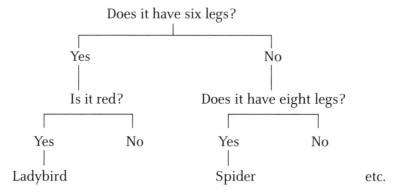

- Use one of the captured creatures as a model for a dice game, with cut-out body parts and numbers. For example, Spider: head = 5, thorax = 4, abdomen = 3, legs = 2 each, eyes = 1 each, any body part = 6 + another turn.
- Devise movements in PE to resemble the movements of a beetle, a butterfly, a snail, a spider. Encourage the children to suggest other animals. Use musical instruments to illustrate the movements.
- Write a story about 'The Spider who had no friends'.
- Debate the issue: 'We should always look after spiders!'
- Brainstorm words about snails and use to create poems.

Points of significant attainment to look for

Children:

- explore animals from a local habitat describing what they observe
- collect data and measurements
- co-operate with each other
- know that animals need food and water to stay alive
- know that there are different species of small creatures/animals
- make comparisons between animals and see patterns
- think aloud by offering speculative explanations for natural phenomena

– show some understanding of why we need to treat animals with care and sensitivity

– begin to be aware of the predator–prey relationship

– use secondary sources, including ICT, to research information about animals.

Additional ideas and resources

- Read: *The Very Hungry Caterpillar* by Eric Carle. Picture Puffin.

                       The Bad-tempered Ladybird by Eric Carle. Picture Puffin.

                       Where the Wild Things are by Maurice Sendak. Picture Lions.

                       Big Bugs by Mary Gribbin and Andrew Tewson. Ladybird.

- Recite: 'Forgiven' (re beetle) in *Now We Are Six* by A. A. Milne. Methuen.

- Sing: 'The snail' in *Sing a Song One* edited by Bird *et al.* Nelson.

- Website: www.thebigbugshow.demon.co.uk

Materials and Their Properties

10. Soggy paper towels
QCA links: 1C, 3C

Introduction

Children grow up in a world where all of the testing and processing of materials has been carried out so that they are presented with the final product: a soft, safe cuddly toy, a fridge magnet, waterproof boots, a fleecy coat. Investigating a range of one type of material not only encourages scientific skills but helps children to understand that tests are necessary and the particular properties of materials makes them useful to us.

Paper has its origin in organic (living) materials, such as wood fibres, rice paper, reeds or fabric. The properties of these long-chain, fibrous molecules enable us to make long, flat, thin pieces of paper or tissue.

Activity

Starting point
Show the children several examples of paper handtowels, from single layer to multi-layer, if possible. An alternative collection could be kitchen paper towels or tissues. (Make sure you have enough examples for several tests.) Begin by asking the children 'How many things can we think of that are made of paper? How many questions can we ask about paper?'

Development
The children may offer several ideas for investigating paper, including mopping up spills or drying hands. Start the investigation by pouring a little water onto the table top (or a plastic cover if necessary). Encourage children to suggest ways of finding out which paper is best for mopping up the water. Ask them to predict what the paper will look like, feel like and how it will behave when it cannot absorb any more water (i.e. when it is saturated). Test how much water each

Table 3.1 How much water can paper towels absorb?

Source of towel	1 tsp (5ml)	2 tsps (10 ml)	3 tsps (15 ml)	4 tsps (20 ml)	
School cloakroom	X	X			
Swimming pool	X				
Town Hall	X	X	X		
DfES cloakroom	X	X	X	X	X

paper towel can absorb using different amounts of water: 1 teaspoon (5 ml), 2 teaspoons (10 ml), 3 teaspoons (15 ml) and 4 teaspoons (20 ml).

Record the results in a grid (see Table 3.1) and use a compatible graphing program (see Useful Resources, e.g. Research Machines 'Starting Graph 1.5') to convert the data into a graph.

Conclusion

Interpret the results and use for a presentation in Sharing Assembly.

Organisation

Work in ability groups of four to five children. For younger or less able children, control the amounts of water and paper (e.g. one teaspoonful of water and whole sheets of paper) so that they can make reasonable comparisons. For more able children, invite them to think of ways themselves to make it a fair comparison (e.g. same area of paper towel, a number of standard teaspoons or millilitres of water).

Questions to encourage thinking skills

- Which is the best paper? Which is the worst? Do we all agree?
- What will it be best for? How can we find out?
- How can we be sure that each paper towel gets the same amount of water? Will that be fair?
- How will we know when the paper towel can't absorb any more water?
- Where do we use paper handtowels? Anywhere else? Why is that, do you think?
- Why do you think manufacturors make different kinds of paper towel?
- What do you think people used before there were any paper towels?

Vocabulary

absorb, absorbency, area, biodegradable, compare, dry, fair test, flammable, manufacturors, measure, predict, rough, saturated ('sopping wet'), smooth, strong, suitable, thick, thin, weak, wet

Units: millilitres (ml)

Extension and enrichment activities

- Design a poster advertising the best paper towels or tissues.

- Compare three or four different washing-up liquids (from poor to good quality). Using rubber gloves, children can help to coat plastic plates (e.g. picnic or toy plates) with vegetable oil and tomato ketchup. Discuss and decide on a measure of washing-up liquid to warm water (e.g. 1 tsp/5 ml to 1/2 cup/100 ml). Which is the best buy and why?

- Investigate four to five different fabrics. Encourage the children to suggest some investigations: e.g. absorbency, easy cut-ability or wearability, flammability.

> **H&S:** Adults need to be in sole charge of the safe burning of very small samples over a sand tray. Discuss why we mustn't wear flammable fabrics near a fire or gas cooker.

- Debate the following problem: (a) We ought to recycle all the paper in our old reading books so we don't have to cut down any more trees; (b) We want to keep our old books so we can read them again and again.

- Find out what the local council does to recycle paper and any other biodegradable materials.

Points of significant attainment to look for

Children:

- collect evidence to answer a question
- make predictions about what might happen
- recognise when a test or comparison is unfair
- describe and record observations and measurements
- help to design investigations
- make simple comparisons and offer explanations as to why something happened
- know about the property of absorbency in different materials
- know that materials are chosen to make particular products because of their properties.

Additional ideas and resources

- Read: *The Do-It-Yourself House that Jack Built.* John Yeoman and Quentin Blake. Puffin.

- Recite: 'This is the house that Jack built' (traditional rhyme).

- Sing: 'The wise man built his house upon the rock' in *Okki Tokki Unga* edited by B. Harrop. A & C Black.

11.   Fur, feathers and fabric
QCA links: 1C, 3C

Introduction

Recognising natural or synthetic materials can be extremely difficult. Many synthetic or man-made materials are so sophisticated that they can confuse us – silk or acetate? wool or fleecy synthetic? fur or fake fur? leather or plastic? cork or composite? The chemistry can explain some of the confusion. Most synthetic fibres are produced from long-chain molecules, which are also a characteristic of natural organic (living) materials. These can give synthetic fabrics comparable qualities such as good insulation, soft texture, water resistance, etc. Then manufacturers add to the confusion by blending natural and synthetic fibres together – look at labels on clothing: '90% polyester + 10% silk'; '95% acetate + 5% cashmere'; 'leather uppers and synthetic soles'. Additionally, natural products that we use in everyday life have been processed in a factory (e.g. wooden pencils, woolly hats), which makes them 'manufactured'. As a result, although we encourage children to know about natural and man-made or synthetic materials, we should not expect them to understand them at this stage.

Activity

Starting point
Tell or read the story of *The Three Little Pigs and the Big Bad Wolf*. Discuss which material was best and why.

Development
Show a collection of materials that includes items made of wood, wool, metal, stone, chalk, stone, cotton, feathers, wax, straw, different plastics (rigid and flexible), small transparent containers of water and vegetable oil, one or two fruits or vegetables, one or two synthetic fabrics, rubber and leather. Use a different selection of five to eight of the items with any group of children. Encourage the children to explore the different materials and then sort them using a variety of criteria. Accept their chosen criteria and if the concept of natural and man-made materials does not arrive that way, have 'your turn', sorting by natural and synthetic. If necessary, explain your choice that some originated from living sources while others were originally made by scientists in laboratories.

Conclusion
After sorting, children choose one natural material and draw a sequence of pictures illustrating the origin of the material and how it is turned into a made object (e.g. woolly coat, pencil, cotton sock). Display the drawings with the materials.

   Now blow up three pink balloons and give them little piggy faces. Use found materials to construct the houses and display the three pigs inside their respective houses.

Organisation

Use mixed ability groups of four to five children. In many instances, more able children will trigger other children's sorting criteria. It might be possible for two groups to sort at the same time as other children draw their ideas of the origins of the pencil, etc.

Questions to encourage thinking skills

- Which things belong together? Why do you think that? What else do they remind you of?
- Which materials would be good for wearing in cold weather? hot weather? for wrapping presents? making furniture?
- Which animals grow fur coats? feathers? Why is that, do you think?
- Where do you think wool comes from? cotton? wood?
- How do you think they collect cotton and turn it into T-shirts? What about other things?
- Why do you think we want scientists to invent these materials? What might happen if we could only have natural materials?

Vocabulary

belong, different, fabric, factory, invent, man-made, manufacture, material, natural, same, scientist, similar, sort, synthetic, use

Extension and enrichment activities

- Arrange a visit to a builder's merchant or a timber yard or a large DIY store to see a range of bricks or timber. With or without a visit, take some samples of bricks or different types of wood into the classroom to explore and investigate. Encourage children to think of appropriate tests for the bricks or timber (e.g. hardness, scratchability, water absorption/'wettability').
- Supply a range of fabrics and make simple clothes for dolls or teddy bears using glue sticks or simple stitching. Use for a classroom display or add prices and use for role play.
- Create a designer label for the dolls' clothes. Make up imaginary bar codes (explain) using thick and thin black felt tip pens. Use a corner of the classroom or the creative-play area to use as a clothes shop.
- Use books, ICT and other resources to research the sources of materials such as granite, silk, gold, pinewood.
- Use books, websites and people and/or a visit to a nearby historical building to find out what kind of clothes people used to wear and what they used to build their houses with long ago. Present the findings.
- Use found materials and natural materials (feathers, cloth, wood, gravel) to make collages of an owl, a magician or a building.

Points of significant attainment to look for

Children:

- sort and classify materials on the basis of simple properties
- know that some materials are found naturally and some are man-made/synthetic
- recognise and name some familiar natural and synthetic materials, such as rocks and plastics
- describe the properties of different materials (e.g. bendy, dull, shiny, solid, rough)
- offer reasonable explanations for the origins and manufacture of familiar items based on existing knowledge and experience
- use knowledge of the properties of materials to suggest suitable uses for them.

Additional ideas and resources

- Read: *The Three Little Pigs and the Big Bad Wolf.* Ladybird Easy Reading Books.
- Recite: 'What are little boys made of?' (traditional rhyme).

  'Hey diddle, dinkety, poppety, pet, The merchants of London they wear scarlet' (traditional rhyme).

  'Wee Willie Winky' (traditional rhyme).

  (All available in *Mother Goose Nursery Rhymes* published by Collins in 1989.)

12.   Cold ice lollies and nice hot tea!
QCA link: 2D

Introduction

Children and adults alike are apt to link insulation with protection from the cold only, whereas insulating materials reduce heat loss or heat gain, that is, *any* heat transfer. Some materials are good conductors of heat (e.g. metals), others are poor conductors (e.g. air, some plastics, thick fabrics). The best non-conductor is a vacuum. We choose materials with known characteristics to serve our purpose: fleecy coats in cold weather, metal saucepans to conduct heat quickly and efficiently. Vacuum flasks usually consist of two flasks, the inner being separated from the outer by a space from which most air has been evacuated. The flasks often have linings that reduce heat transfer too. Thus vacuum flasks can keep tea hot, or milk cold. Discuss the concept cartoon of the snowman and his coat (see Figure 3.1) before and after the investigation – will the snowman melt more quickly with or without the coat or will it make no difference?

Figure 3.1 Snowman (Naylor and Keogh 2000)

Activity

Starting point

Buy a packet of ice lollies or prepare something similar with diluted fruit squash frozen solid in plastic cups or yogurt pots. Assemble a range of test materials: paper, plastic bags, wood pieces, kitchen foil, bubble wrap, thin cotton fabric and thick fleecy/woolly fabric. Invite the children to feel and describe the lollies or pots.

Development

Discuss and ask the children to predict which material(s), when wrapped around the lollies, will keep them frozen until after playtime or another chosen time (see Figure 3.2). Which materials will allow the lollies to melt? Encourage the children to think how they can test their predictions. They need to decide how many layers of each test material should be used and how they should cover each pot or lolly to be sure that the test is fair. (NB: Put all pots in the same place.)

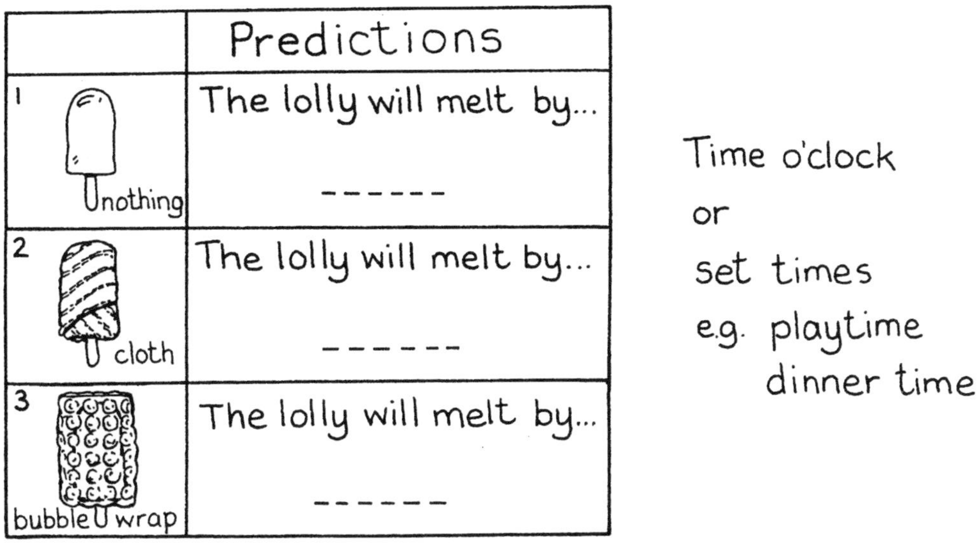

		Predictions
1	*nothing*	The lolly will melt by... ------
2	*cloth*	The lolly will melt by... ------
3	*bubble wrap*	The lolly will melt by... ------

Time o'clock
or
set times
e.g. playtime
      dinner time

Figure 3.2 Predicting which material is the best insulator

Have the children set up the investigation and check the lollies each half hour, recording the results, until the specified time. This may not be accurate but it develops children's skills of estimating and compromising.

Conclusion

Complete any recording sheets. Able children could write explanations as to why some materials were good insulators. Agree the order of best to worst materials for insulating/keeping ice cold, then eat the lollies or prepare slushy fruit ice to drink through straws (semi-frozen squash).

Organisation

Work in mixed ability groups of four children. If the investigation is to be carried out one group at a time, use four lollies for comparison. If the whole class is carrying out the work, each group could have two lollies for comparison and pool data in the plenary session.

Questions to encourage thinking skills

- Which material do you think will be best for keeping the ice frozen? for keeping a cup of tea nice and hot?
- Which things do we like to eat cold? Why is that?
- Can you think why some foods have to be kept cold in the fridge?
- Which things do we like to eat when they are hot? Why is that?
- Can you think why some foods have to be heated up for safety?
- Which materials do we use in cold winter weather to keep ourselves warm?
- Which materials do we use in hot weather to keep ourselves cool?

Extension and enrichment activities

● Carry out a similar test on pretend 'tea', using hand-hot water poured into jars with lids. Test by hand or thermometer (children may need training in the use of these) before selecting materials to wrap around, above and below the jars, in a fair test. Seal with sticky tape or string (the tighter the better). Test every 20 minutes by hand or thermometer. The time spent between tests can be used to complete writing frames, such as 'We think that the jar with .... will stay hot longer'.

● Children can write down or give verbal instructions as to 'How to build a snowman'.

● Discuss 'Snowman' No. 8.2 in *Concept Cartoons in Science Education* by Stuart Naylor and Brenda Keogh (2000), as shown in Figure 3.1.

● On a large piece of card, draw a board game with a winding track and numbered squares. Highlight some of the squares and cut out a set of blank cards. Encourage more able children to draw some pictures of hot objects on some cards and cold objects on others. Use dice to play the game and when a player lands on a highlighted square they pick up a card. A hot card takes a player forward three squares, a cold card back two squares.

Points of significant attainment to look for

Children:

– respond to questions about heating and cooling and seek answers using first-hand experience

– make predictions based on existing experience

– help to plan investigations

– collect data and use it to draw conclusions

– offer reasonable explanations based on experience for why things cool down.

Vocabulary

cold, cool, fabric, freeze, frozen, heat, hot, insulate, lose, lost, material, retain, temperature, test, thermometer

Units: degrees Celsius (°C)

Additional ideas and resources

● Read: *The Snowman* by Raymond Briggs. Puffin Books.

● Recite: 'The North wind doth blow' (traditional rhyme).

    'Doctor Foster went to Gloucester' (traditional rhyme).

● Website: www.conceptcartoons.com

13. Mixed up materials
QCA links: 1C, 3C

Introduction

Some materials are readily identifiable as solids (rigid structure) and others as liquids (they flow). However some substances are less easy to classify: salt grains and powdered flour 'pour' and hummus and mashed potato are 'squashy'. Cornflour, when mixed with a certain amount of water behaves like both a liquid (runny) and a solid (cracks).

Mixtures can be:

solids + solids (raisins and lentils, raisins and flour)

solids + liquids (some separate, e.g. raisins sink in water; some make a solution, e.g. salt dissolves in water; and some exist as a suspension (e.g. flour disperses in water)

liquids + liquids (washing-up liquid in water, oil in water – oil will float)

gases + solids (meringue)

gases + liquids (carbonated water)

gases + gases (air)

In a mixture, we can separate the ingredients by sieving, filtering, evaporating, etc. Sometimes the ingredients react to each other chemically, e.g. bicarbonate of soda in vinegar.

Experiments with materials will start to make children familiar with a range of physical characteristics and scientific vocabulary so that then, or later, classifying materials makes sense.

Activity

Starting point

Set a problem to solve with the story: 'Look! Yesterday I dropped my shopping and mixed up all the salt, lentils, flour and raisins (show tray of mixed items). Can you think of a way to separate them out?' Accept the children's suggestions (pick out, sieve, dissolve) and test them.

> **H&S:** Remind children that some of the substances in the kitchen are dangerous and shouldn't be touched, smelt or tasted (e.g. cleaning fluids). The rule is 'Always ask a grown-up if it is safe to touch'.

Development

Display some familiar kitchen materials in separate transparent containers, such as water, vegetable oil, white vinegar, syrup, salt, sugar, self-raising flour, wholegrain flour, cornflour, raisins, lentils, bicarbonate of soda (baking powder), hummus, cornflakes, cheese. Use a smaller selection for younger children.

Figure 3.3 Mixing materials

> **H&S:** The substances are all foods so they should be safe to touch and taste. Nevertheless, encourage the children to taste in very tiny quantities or by dipping the tip of the little finger in. Children who do not want to taste or smell should not be coerced – they are more likely to join in eventually if their anxieties are respected early on.

Encourage children to use their senses to describe the different substances and predict what might happen if they get mixed up. Try mixing up solid + solid, solid + liquid and liquid + liquid (see Figure 3.3). For younger children, make just one mixture. Investigate the solubility of one solid in different liquids, e.g. salt in water, vinegar, oil. Encourage children to ask their own questions comparing the similarities and differences between materials.

Conclusion

Write down the descriptive words used by the children for later reflection and use in poems.

Organisation

Use groups of four or five children in ability groups. Each group could have a slightly different selection of materials to observe and investigate. Pool ideas in the plenary.

Able children could try several investigations and use more sophisticated methods of measuring, e.g. instead of spoonfuls measure in grams, and instead of half a cupful measure 100 millilitres.

Questions to encourage thinking skills

- What do you notice about the materials? Anything else?
- What do you think they will feel like? smell like? taste like? How can we test them safely?
- How do you think we can sort them? Any other way?

- What do you think will happen if we put some of them into water?
- Will it be the same if we put them into oil? or vinegar?
- What makes you think that?
- How can we make sure that the amounts we put in are the same?
- Do you think the salt/sugar is still there in the water – even though it seems to have disappeared? How can we find out?
- Can you think of any way we might get the salt back again?

Vocabulary

bubbles of gas, crystals, disperse, dissolve, float, flow, grains, hard, liquid, materials, mix, mixture, powder, rough, round, runny, shiny, sink, smooth, soft, solid, solubility, solute, solution, solvent, squashy, suspension, wrinkled

Units: weight: grams (g)   capacity: millilitres (ml)

Extension and enrichment ideas

- Add spoonfuls of salt to a jar of water, stirring until no more salt will dissolve and a small residue lies on the bottom of the jar (i.e. it is a supersaturated solution). Attach a piece of knotted string to a pencil and suspend over the salt solution so that the knot is well under the water. Stand the jar in a warm place. The salt will crystallise out of the evaporating water. You may even see transparent cubic crystals of salt (by eye, handlens or microscope) before the salt effloresces (goes white and crusty on exposure to air).
- Set another problem to solve: separate the nuggets of chocolate (avoid nuts) in chocolate chip cookie biscuits. (Possible solutions include crumbling, sieving or heating so the chocolate melts.) Discuss the comparison between this and mining metallic ores from rock.
- Most able children might draw what they imagine is happening when something 'dissolves' and/or offer their imaginative explanations.
- Discuss 'Salty water' No. 9.1 in *Concept Cartoons in Science Education* by Stuart Naylor and Brenda Keogh (2000), as shown in Figure 3.4.
- Write a story beginning 'Once upon a time the sea had no salt in it. Then one day . . .' or draw a sequence of pictures to illustrate such a story.

Points of significant attainment to look for

Children:

- use senses to explore and describe the similarities and differences between materials
- ask questions about and sort the materials on the basis of simple physical properties
- begin to discuss the meanings of dissolving and solubility
- make predictions about what might happen to materials when mixed together

Figure 3.4 Salty water (Naylor and Keogh 2000)

- know how to behave safely regarding foods and household materials
- record observations and measurements
- make simple comparisons and offer explanations as to why something happened
- recognise some of the differences between solids and liquids.

Additional ideas and resources

● Read: 'How the sea became salty' in *Aesop's Fables* translated from Latin by Lava Gibbs. Oxford World Classics, Oxford University Press.

14. How attractive!
QCA link: 3E

Introduction

We are surrounded by and subject to a range of invisible forces all the time: gravity, friction, air pressure, blood pressure, etc. Magnetic force is also 'invisible' but its effects are easier to see and discuss as well as being exciting and fun. As far as learning objectives listed in national curricula are concerned, the study of magnets is included in 'Materials and their properties' which demonstrates the difficulty of labelling concepts that overlap more than one area.

Magnetism is a force that occurs when the north–south poles of atoms in iron in particular, or an electrical current, are all aligned in the same direction. This has a cumulative effect and creates a force field around it, whereby other nearby materials made of atoms that have polarity too (e.g. metals) are attracted or repelled. Unlike poles attract, like poles repel.

It is essential that children have access to very good quality magnets to explore magnetism and see the two aspects of the force – the push as well as the pull. An old degraded magnet that can barely pick up two or three paper clips is not worth keeping.

Activity

Starting point

Set up a problem for the children to solve by attaching a long cotton thread to a small cylindrical magnet and suspending it above a strong ring magnet on the floor or table top (ring magnets are polarised on each flat surface), as shown in Figure 3.5. Set the small magnet swinging and watch it wobble as it passes over the ring magnet. Ask the children why it is behaving in this way. For added suspense, before the children see this phenomenon, cover the ring magnet with sugar paper and invite the children to offer any explanations for the movement.

Development

(a) Investigating magnetic materials – Sort and classify a range of objects, including those made from metal (keys, paper clips, bulldog clips, nails, pieces of jewellery on temporary loan), plastic, wood and paper, and fabrics. Introduce a

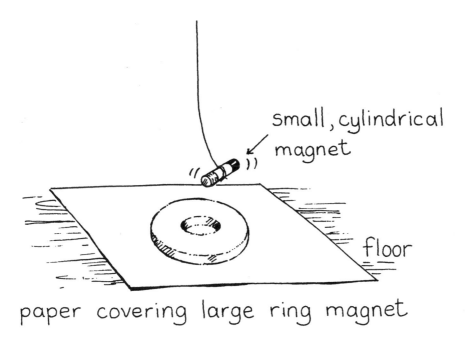

Figure 3.5 Why does the small cylindrical magnet 'wobble' over the large ring magnet?

good strong magnet and encourage the children to predict which materials will 'stick' to the magnet. Invite explanations as to why this might happen, then introduce other materials to confirm or challenge these. Display the results in Venn hoops.

(b) Investigating magnetism as a force – Use a range of magnets of varying strengths and shapes. Invite the children to predict how each magnet will behave towards the others (pushing and pulling/attracting and repelling). Discuss this, then encourage the children to devise a way of measuring the strengths of the magnets (e.g. how far it repels another magnet/how many paper clips it can attract).

Conclusion

Display the sorted materials from (a) in Venn hoops together with a challenge: 'Is there any other way we can sort them (e.g. by colour, size, shape etc.)?

Organisation

After the introductory discussion, work in ability groups of four or five children.

Questions to encourage thinking skills

- Which objects belong together? Why have you put those ones together?
- Is there any other way we can sort them?
- Which ones will belong together if we sort them with a magnet? Why is that, do you think?
- Will all magnets work in the same way?
- Are some magnets stronger than others? How can we find out?
- Which ones pulled the most? pushed the most?
- Does magnetism work through paper? cloth? a table top?
- How do you think a magnet works?

Vocabulary

attract, attraction, distance, explain, fabric, filings, iron, magnet, magnetic, magnetism, material, metal, non-metal, north, north-seeking, object, pole, predict, pull, push, repel, repulsion, south, strong, stronger, strongest, weak

Extension and enrichment activities

- Discuss 'Magnets' No. 11.3 in *Concept Cartoons in Science Education* by Stuart Naylor and Brenda Keogh (2000), as shown in Figure 3.6.
- Devise magnetic games, for example, draw a track or maze onto a cardboard box lid and use paper clips and a magnet underneath to drag the paper clip around the course (see Figure 3.7). Think of obstacles to add to the course (a hill, a tunnel, a fence).

Figure 3.6 Magnets (Naylor and Keogh 2000)

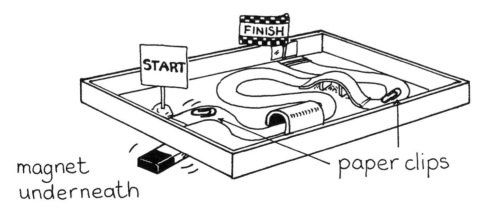

Figure 3.7 A magnetic game

- Dramatise magnetism in a movement or game indicating push/pull, attract/repel.
- Set up a table with a vertical metal tray and bring in fridge magnets to display and discuss.
- Look at a real compass which always points to magnetic north. Encourage explanations for magnetism and the behaviour of a compass needle.

Points of significant attainment to look for

Children:

- sort and classify metals on the basis of simple properties
- describe the properties of different metals (e.g. magnetic, dull, shiny, solid, rough)
- know that some materials are attracted by magnets and others are not
- know that magnetism is a kind of force and can attract and repel
- offer reasonable explanations for the origins and manufacture of familiar items based on existing knowledge and experience
- carry out an investigation to measure the strength of different magnets.

Additional ideas and resources

- Glue a piece of dowelling to a wooden base. Add ring magnets over the dowelling in order of polarity such that the force of each lower magnet repels the one above. The magnets will seem to defy gravity by 'floating' above each other – in fact the forces are in equilibrium as the strength of the repelling force is equal to the downward force of gravity.

---

15. Porridge and pancakes
QCA link: 3C

Introduction

The concept targeted here is that when some materials are heated there is irreversible change. Change occurs when materials combine to become new materials or when the material is permanently degraded. This is different from a change of state where the material stays the same but changes from solid to liquid or from liquid to gas, or the reverse (see Activity 16, Air, ice and water).

Many children's stories and rhymes are based on cereal crops simply because these are life-preserving, staple foods. In many periods of history, from Scotland to China, people have even been paid in oats, wheat or rice.

H&S: Remind children to wash their hands before handling food and why.

Activity A: Porridge

Starting point

Read the story of *The Magic Porridge Pot* (which keeps on making porridge until it fills the town) or *Goldilocks and the Three Bears* (porridge that was too hot, too cold, just right).

Development

Explore some porridge oats using all the senses. Invite predictions as to what might happen when the oats are mixed with water and cooked. Weigh or measure out one cupful of oats (75 g) to two cupfuls of water (500 ml) and place in a saucepan, add a pinch of salt and cook over a low heat, stirring gently all the time until the porridge thickens. Invite the children to look at the oats now – without touching! Allow to cool, then serve in small quantities. Children could choose to add either a spoonful of honey or sugar or syrup and a little milk. Discuss the changes that occurred.

More able children could calculate:

(a) how many cupfuls or grams of oats are needed to make porridge for the whole class if one cupful/75 g makes enough porridge for five children;

(b) if 75 g of oats need 500 ml water, how many millilitres would be needed to make porridge for the whole class.

Activity B: Pancakes

Starting point

Read the story of *The Big Pancake* retold by N. Baxter (Ladybird) which was eaten by the fox when crossing the river, just as in the story of *The Little Gingerbread Boy* (traditional, Ladybird Easy Reading Books).

Development

Set out self-raising flour, salt, eggs, water and milk (self-raising flour makes a lighter pancake than plain flour). Crack one of the eggs into a basin. Explore and discuss the nature of the ingredients and predict possible changes on heating.

Set out plates, knives and forks and bowls of toppings, such as (a) soft margarine, sugar and lemon juice or (b) soft-scoop ice-cream.

Put one cupful of self-raising flour (100 g) and a pinch of salt into a large bowl. Make a well in the middle and add half a cupful of milk mixed with water (200–250 ml). Crack an egg into this and stir the mixture. Gradually beat more firmly, adding a little extra water if needed to produce a thin, creamy consistency.

Put a little vegetable oil into a frying pan, bring to heat, then pour in approximately half a tablespoon of mixture. Tilt the pan to spread a thin layer of mixture and cook the first side quickly. When the top surface bubbles, toss or turn the pancake with a spatula and cook the second side more slowly. Turn onto a plate: one pancake is enough for two children to dress with either topping (a) or (b), roll up or fold into half, cut and eat.

More able children could calculate how many grams of flour are needed for the whole class if 100 g make enough pancakes for four or five children.

Conclusion

The teacher or children write out and decorate the recipe/s by hand or computer (word processing and clip art). Photocopy enough for all children to illustrate one and take home.

Organisation

Work in friendship groups of four to six children to explore the ingredients, help prepare and eat the foods. Allow children to refuse to eat the porridge or pancakes if they wish.

Questions to encourage thinking skills

- What do you notice about these ingredients?
- Can you guess where oats come from? wheat flour?
- What do you think will happen when we cook it?
- Why do you think the porridge/a pancake bubbles when it is hot?
- What has happened to the ingredients now? Why do you think that?
- What else can you think of that changes when it gets cooked?
- Do you think we could get the oats/egg back? Why not?
- What might happen to us if we touch very hot pans? Why might that be?
- People have lived on cereals like wheat, oats or rice for thousands of years. Can you guess why cereal crops are so important to us?

Vocabulary

cereals, change, consistency, cool, hard, heat, hot, ingredients, liquid, material, predict, recipe, runny, soft, solid

Units: grams (g) millilitres (ml)

Extension and enrichment activities

- Dramatise one of the stories about porridge and pancakes. Add a musical accompaniment and show in Sharing Assembly.
- Create a bar chart of children's favourite dishes (e.g. curry, cake, jelly, chicken and chips).
- Make a display of different kinds of bread. Use after a few days or dispose of safely.
- Draw imaginary pictures of where oats or wheat flour might come from.
- Talk about or write a story about what was happening to the poor hungry fox before the pancake came along.

Points of significant attainment to look for

Children:

- explore and describe different materials/ingredients using the senses
- show some understanding of why we need to wash hands before handling food and behave safely near heating appliances
- make predictions about possible changes to materials when heated
- describe the way the ingredients changed when heated
- offer explanations for change based on existing knowledge and first-hand experience
- know that heat can change materials
- know that some changes are irreversible.

Additional ideas and resources

- Turn the role-play area into a snack bar or crêperie (French pancakes).
- Make thin, modelling-clay pancakes and use with a play frying pan to practise tossing. Discuss what healthy foods and vegetarian meals (using found materials) the snack bar might offer too.
- Read: *The Big Pancake* retold by N. Baxter. Ladybird Books.

  The Little Gingerbread Boy. Ladybird Easy Reading Books.

  The Magic Porridge Pot. Ladybird Easy Reading Books.

  Don't Forget the Bacon by Pat Hutchins. Picture Puffin.

  The Pooh Cook Book by Katie Stewart and E. H. Shepard. Magnet Books.

  The Tiger Who Came to Tea by Judith Kerr. Picture Lions.

  Goldilocks and the Three Bears. Ladybird Easy Reading Books.

- Recite: 'Rice pudding' in *When We Were Very Young* by A. A. Milne. Methuen.

16.   Air, ice and water
QCA links: 2D, 3C

Introduction

Children often confuse melting with dissolving. Repeat experiences are needed to reinforce the separate concepts. Change of state occurs when a material gains enough energy to move from a solid state to liquid and then to a gas, or when it loses energy and the process is reversed. The two factors influencing change of state are temperature and pressure, but with younger children we ignore the latter and assume that all the changes are taking place at normal atmospheric pressure.

Materials have different melting and boiling points (e.g. water, wax, oil, steel, oxygen, carbon dioxide, plastics) and the process begins at the surface of the material. Water acts as a yardstick for comparison, with ice melting at 0°C and liquid water evaporating and becoming water vapour (steam) at 100°C. Nevertheless, the process begins on either side of these temperatures and, in particular, water begins to crystallise at 4°C and, as ice is less dense than water, the ice floats. This means that ponds and seas freeze from the surface downwards, and as the ice acts as an insulating material, this process allows living things to carry on living below the surface.

Activity

Starting point

Set up a balloon filled with water and frozen in the freezer for two to three days and bring in a helium balloon. Invite as many questions as possible about the balloons and their contents.

Development

(a) Investigating changes of state – Compare three states of matter using three balloons: one full of air (gas), another full of water (liquid) and the third one the ice balloon (solid). Encourage the children to explore the balloons by sight and touch. Try squeezing them gently, then drop them gently from a low height into a bowl or transparent water tank. Discuss the behaviour. Try floating the three balloons in a tank of water (see Figure 3.8). Finally, 'pop' the balloons over a bowl or tank and discuss what happens.

(b) Solid, liquid or gas? – Have materials ready that represent three different states: bricks, metal spoon, plastic spoon, vegetable oil, candle, chocolate, ink, balloon + air, helium balloon, sand, eye dropper and straw (both contain air).

Ask the children to sort the objects by any criteria as well as by solid/liquid/gas (or 'air'). Discuss the full balloon, eye dropper and straw and what is inside. The eye dropper and straw can be squeezed or blown under water to show bubbles emerging.

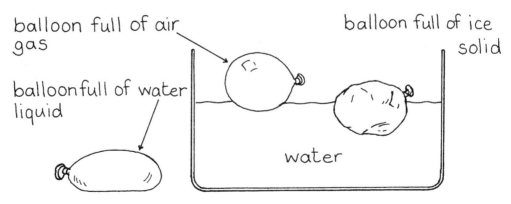

Figure 3.8 Solid, liquid and gas – will they float?

Conclusion

Children draw or write a list of objects that are solid, liquid or gas.

Organisation

Introduce the activities as a whole class, then use ability groups of four or five children to explore and sort the materials.

Questions to encourage thinking skills

- What do you notice about each balloon?

- How does each balloon behave when dropped? in the water? popped?

- What do you think is inside the full balloon? eye dropper? straw? How can we find out?

- What do you think are the differences between a liquid and a solid?

- What does sand count as?

- How do you think we could turn the ice into water?

- How could we turn the water into water vapour – safely?

Vocabulary

air, boil, cold, condense, cool, freeze, gas, hard, ice, liquid, material, melt, rigid, runny, soft, warm, warmth, water vapour

Extension and enrichment activities

- Discuss changing ice into water and water into water vapour. Children could choose locations for melting ice cubes to investigate the effect of warmth/heat.

- Gently boil some water in a saucepan and show that the water vapour is still water by condensing some on a cold metal saucepan placed nearby.

- Make ice sculptures by filling different plastic shapes with water, seal off tightly and freeze into solid ice: e.g. rubber glove, plastic food bag pushed down into a sock, plastic food bag pushed into half a grapefruit or coconut. Display in a tray and time how long each one takes to melt.

- Mix cornflour with enough water to make it behave as a solid (cracks) and a liquid (flows). Discuss the behaviour.

- Discuss 'Liquids' No. 8.4 in *Concept Cartoons in Science Education* by Stuart Naylor and Brenda Keogh (2000), as shown in Figure 3.9.

- Design a safety poster: 'Do not play on the ice'.

- Use white paints or chalks on black sugar paper to create a picture of 'The land of ice and snow'.

Figure 3.9 Liquids (Naylor and Keogh 2000)

Points of significant attainment to look for

Children:

- suggest possible investigations to find answers to questions about different materials
- sort and classify materials by different criteria including different states of matter
- describe what happens when materials are heated and cooled

- use scientific vocabulary in a meaningful way
- know that some materials can 'change back' (i.e. reversible change), such as water freezing into ice and melting into water, water evaporating into water vapour (gas) and condensing back into water
- know that temperature is a measure of how hot or cold something is.

Additional ideas and resources

- Read: *The Snowman* by Raymond Briggs. Puffin Books.

Physical Processes

17. Lighting up!
QCA link: 2F

Introduction

(NB: This introduction to electricity also applies to Activity 18, Good conductors.)

Prior to the introduction of statutory and non-statutory documents for science (e.g. National Curriculum [Engand], DfEE QCA 1998), many of us taught electricity successfully to children of five to seven years and also to children in nursery and reception classes. There are two major reasons why young children should be taught about electricity: (a) children living in developed countries are surrounded by, and use electrical appliances, and (b) when children learn that even 4 volts can make a light bulb glow bright and feel quite hot, they develop a healthier respect for the potential dangers of mains electricity at 220/240 volts (= A LOT of electricity!).

Nevertheless, there are two conditions to abide by when teaching electricity to young children:

1. It is not necessary for them to understand the concepts – knowledge is sufficient.

2. Good appropriate resources are essential. It is no use attempting to teach electricity to young children with nothing more than bare wires, crocodile clips, a loose battery and loose bulbs. We are not using this as an exercise in testing fine motor skills (i.e. the ability to use a crocodile clip). A good mounted set of devices with banana clip connections (e.g. 5–13 Electricity – Constructional Kits) is essential. Such kits usually work with three 1.5 volt batteries, perfectly safely.

With these provisos, children are delighted to learn about electricity and how it makes things work. (NB: Static electricity is interesting but the concepts are even more complex than current electricity.)

Activity

Starting point

(NB: All devices should be mounted, including the battery holder and the batteries.)

It is worth repeating the following activities even if the children have explored electricity before. Repetition reminds and reinforces existing concepts and allows for further development. Begin with questions such as 'How many things can we all think of that use electricity?' and 'How many questions can we all think of to ask about electricity?' Then present children with the following: battery holder with batteries in place, bulb, switch and wires with banana clip ends. Allow free exploration in making the bulb light up. If the battery box is ignored, suggest including this in the circuit, then discuss why it was necessary.

> **H&S:** Train children to check that the batteries are all aligned in the same direction.

Development

Encourage the children to look at and feel (with caution) the light bulb. Explain that the amount of electricity in the batteries is equal to about 4 volts. If 4 volts can make a little bulb hot, what do the children think 200 volts might do? (burn, break, burst, etc.)

> **H&S:** Warn that mains electricity is more than 200 volts and that they should *never* touch three-pin wall plugs or wires on electrical appliances.

Give each child a banana clip wire. Make a 'touch-ring' back to the battery box connected to the bulb. Will the bulb light up without the switch? What might happen if someone breaks the chain? What happens now? With a good electricity kit, you will be able to remove the switch cover and see how it works by breaking the circuit.

Replace the light bulb with a buzzer. Ask for predictions as to what this device can do. Try it out. (NB: Buzzers are usually one-way devices and won't work when reversed in a circuit.)

Conclusion

Dramatise circuits in a ring of children – pass the squeeze around the ring to light up a bulb (child smiles) or a buzzer (child buzzes).

Organisation

Use social or ability groups of four or five children. The questions will challenge the thinking skills of the more able children and their responses will prompt the subsequent question or enrichment activity. It is important that in the first exploratory exercise, the devices are limited to focus thinking. Subsequent exploratory activities need to be resourced such that each group of two or three children has enough equipment for their own circuit to ensure every child is involved in first-hand experience.

Questions to encourage thinking skills

- What do you notice about the bulb? Anything else?
- What do you think is inside the battery? (Do not cut open as this is unsafe.)
- What might happen if we connect even more wires into a circuit in a 'touch-ring'? (With enough wires, the bulb dims due to increased resistance in the wires.)
- What does the switch look like inside? How do you think it works?
- Which places do we really need to have electric lights? Anywhere else?
- Which places do we need to have buzzers? Why?
- Can you find out what people used before we had electricity and electric lights?
- Why should we never touch mains wall plugs and wires on electrical appliances?

Vocabulary

appliances, banana clip, battery, bright, bulb, buzzer, circuit, connect, connection, danger, device, electricity, light, mains, switch, volts (volts 'push' electricity round the circuit), wire

Units: volts (v)

Extension and enrichment activities

- Discuss 'Switch' No.10.1 in *Concept Cartoons in Science Education* by Stuart Naylor and Brenda Keogh (2000), as shown in Figure 4.1.
- Use mixed media and materials (e.g. string, small boxes, kitchen roll tubes, shiny paper, bubble wrap, etc.) to make a three-dimensional representation of a circuit and lit bulb or buzzer.
- Use the circuit and devices to light up a doll's house, a shoe box house or a large model of a police car or ambulance made from found materials.
- Discuss the Morse code. Some children could design their own codes for 'Help', 'Playtime', 'Sit down', etc. and use a circuit with bulb (silent) or buzzer to present their symbols to the class and/or involve others in using them appropriately.
- Some children could carry out research to find out who invented the light bulb and make a presentation of their findings to others.

Figure 4.1 Switch (Naylor and Keogh 2000)

Points of significant attainment to look for

Children:

- observe and describe events using simple scientific vocabulary
- use simple equipment safely
- are aware of health hazards in the home (PSHE)
- make simple predictions, carry out tests and offer explanations for what they found out
- know that electricity can make different devices work
- know that a switch is a way of breaking an electrical circuit so that devices stop working.

Additional ideas and resources

- Rig up a circuit at the entrance to the classroom so that people entering will have to switch on a light or a buzzer (can be noisy but fun!).
- Contact the Understanding Electricity Educational Service, 30 Millbank, London SW1 4RD for resources (some are free to schools).
- Buy a good electricity kit for younger children, such as 5–13 Electricity – Constructional Kits from PO Box 513, Hertford, SG14 3PH.

18. Good conductors
QCA links: 3A, 3F

Introduction

(See introduction to Activity 17, Lighting up!).

Children who are already exploring simple electrical circuits are also capable of exploring conductivity in materials. Nursery children taught by the author could explain that when there was a break in the circuit (i.e. a switch), not only would the bulb not light up but the gap could be closed by using a metal key, a drinks can and kitchen foil, but not by cloth, paper or wood.

Conductivity describes the property of some materials to conduct an electrical current easily. Generally speaking, most metals conduct well (they have ions that become polarised – see the discussion on magnetism in Activity 14, How attractive!). Organic materials usually conduct poorly (the molecules usually have covalent bonds) with the exception of carbon, which conducts electricity well. However, if there is enough electricity (e.g. lightning), electricity can go through air, rock and stone, wood, fabric and the human body. Lightning conductors on the sides of tall brick buildings attract the electricity to avoid the destructive discharge through the building materials.

Activity

Starting point
Set up a simple electrical circuit including a battery box, wires and a bulb or buzzer (as in Activity 17, Lighting up!). Start by joining up the circuit to light a bulb or buzzer, then create a gap between two wires ending with banana clips or crocodile clips. Invite the children to suggest which materials might complete the circuit and conduct the electricity to the bulb.

Development
Use a range of different materials found in the school or classroom, such as a plastic pen, wooden pencil, glass jar, sock, keys, kitchen foil, etc., and test the materials to see if they can complete the circuit and make the bulb or buzzer work.

Conclusion
Draw or make a written list of the materials that do conduct easily and those that do not.

> **H&S:** Remind the children again that they should *never* touch wires or plugs in mains electricity or household appliances. The classroom circuits use just a little bit of electricity whereas mains electricity uses an enormous amount – the difference between the two is like the difference between sliding down a slide and falling out of an aeroplane without a parachute.

Organisation

Work in friendship groups of four or five children, using a slightly different group of materials each time. In the plenary discussion, discuss the common features of the materials that successfully closed the gap in the circuit.

Questions to encourage thinking skills

- Will the bulb light up if we make a gap in the circuit? Why not?
- Which materials might be best for closing the gap? Why do you think that?
- Which materials conducted the electric current easily?
- Which materials didn't conduct the electricity easily?
- Which materials should we use for wires to carry electricity?
- Which materials should we use to protect us from an electric current?
- What dangers might happen to us if we touched wires or mains plugs?

Vocabulary

banana clip, battery, break, buzzer, circuit, complete, connect, connection, crocodile clip, current, electric, electricity, foil, gap, work

Extension and enrichment activities

- Design a poster reminding everyone not to touch electric plugs or wires in the home.
- Make individual or group choice cards. Cut pieces of card approximately 20 cm × 15 cm (or 30 cm × 20 cm for a group card). Punch an equal number of matching holes down each side of the card. Choose a theme for the card: matching words and pictures, numerals and objects, questions and answers. Write the first question at the side of the first hole on the left-hand side and write the answer on a non-matching hole on the right-hand side. On the reverse of the card, join these holes together with a strip of folded kitchen foil, then insulate the strip with masking or sticky tape. Repeat this process with question on the left-hand side and answer in a non-matching hole on the right until all the holes are used up. Play the game by connecting the card to an electric circuit, using it as the gap in the circuit. Children have to answer each question in turn, connecting one clipped wire with the question and the other with the answer. If the answer is correct the circuit is completed and the bulb lights up (see Figure 4.2).
- Design and make a dinosaur trap or burglar alarm. Inside a cardboard box, use simple equipment to set up an electrical circuit as in the main activity, leaving a gap between two clipped wires. Attach a piece of kitchen foil to one clip, folded two or three times to make the foil strong enough to stay slightly raised above the other clip. Use a plastic or modelling clay dinosaur or burglar, heavy enough to tread onto the foil and complete the circuit triggering the light or buzzer. Finish by decorating the box to resemble either a forest or a house.

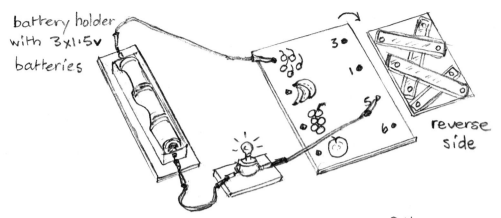

battery holder with 3×1·5v batteries

3
1
5
6
reverse side

Connect the holes underneath with kitchen foil and insulate each one with sticky tape.

Figure 4.2 A choice card

Points of significant attainment to look for

Children:

- respond to questions about circuits and use first-hand experience to find answers to some of them
- make predictions about which materials make good or bad conductors
- follow simple instructions to control risks to themselves and others
- know of the dangers of household electrical appliances and how to behave safely
- know that switches can close or make a gap in a circuit
- offer explanations to others about what happened.

Additional Ideas and resources

- Obtain *Good Cooking* and other publications from the Understanding Electricity Educational Service, 30 Millbank, London SW1 4RD.

19. Do red things float?
QCA link: 3C

Introduction

Children explore floating objects from baby bathtimes. The concepts involved in floating and sinking are a little complex but it is important to continue the exploration without expecting full understanding at this stage. The forces operating on objects in water are gravity (downwards) and upthrust from the water (upwards).

An object floats if its overall density (including what may be inside it) is less than that of the same volume of water. Equally, an object will sink if its overall density is greater than the same volume of water. The overall density of a wooden boat (less dense than water) filled with iron canons (more dense than water) would make it sink, while an iron boat (more dense than water) filled with wooden furniture and air (less dense than water) will make it float. Density of materials is calculated on the weight per unit volume.

Activity

Starting point

This activity elicits children's existing knowledge or assumptions and challenges these. Collect a wide range of objects to investigate, particularly red things that float, for example: a cork, paper clip, red plastic counter, wooden brick, red Lego brick, stone, little red toy, red apple, red balloon, pear (sinks), red plastic lid. Create a 'predict and record' result sheet like the one shown in Figure 4.3 and photocopy it for use for class, group or individual predictions.

Development

Fill a transparent tank with water. Encourage the children to make predictions before each red or non-red object is put into the tank. Repeat with five or six red

Figure 4.3 A predict and record results sheet

floaters and two or three non-red sinkers, then ask what the children notice and why they think that. Then produce a non-red floater (e.g. a green Lego brick) and a red sinker (e.g. a red painted metal clip) and test these. Ask for the children's revised explanations. Introduce other floaters and sinkers. Children then sort the objects and give as many reasons as they can think of as to why some objects float.

Conclusion

Complete the 'predict and record' results sheets for other objects. Able children could write an explanation of what 'floating' means.

Organisation

Use social groups of four or five, with children taking turns at predicting and testing the objects. Sorting can be recorded by drawings. Able children could add written explanations for their group. More able children can then carry out extension activities and make a presentation of their findings to the class.

Questions to encourage thinking skills

- Do all the floaters float in the same way? To the same depth? Are some higher out of the water than the others? Why might that be?
- If you push a floater downwards, will it sink?
- Will the objects float better or worse in salty water? How can we find out?
- Would a coconut float or sink? Why? How can we find out? What about other nuts?
- Why do you think that fish don't sink? How can we find out?
- How do you think submarines go down under the water and come back up again?

Vocabulary

air, deep, dense, density, depth, explain, float, force, greater than, ice, less than, material, predict, pressure, push, sink, suspended

Extension and enrichment activities

- Make floating things sink. Use floaters such as plastic or wooden boats, stable plastic dishes or lids (yogurt pots tip up). Children predict as many ways as they can think of to make them sink, then try their ideas out (where safe). Use the plenary discussion for children to describe and explain what they did and what happened.
- Make sinking objects float (kitchen foil and modelling clay): demonstrate how a crumpled up piece of foil or a lump of modelling clay will sink in the tank (see Figure 4.4). Can the children make the foil float enough to support a plastic toy? Can it support two toys? Can they do the same with the

Figure 4.4 Making sinking objects float

modelling clay? (This is more tricky as clay breaks up into pieces when very wet. If this happens discard it and use new clay.) Discuss, describe and explain what happened.

- Demonstrate and compare how an ice balloon (balloon filled with water and frozen in a freezer for two or three days) and a water balloon float in water. What is the same? What is different? Why might that be?

- Ask more able children to create a story: 'When I was swimming underwater, I found the pirate's treasure. The gold and silver were too heavy to carry. I had to make them float. I decided to . . .'.

- Encourage more able children to think of and draw or write down as many things as possible that float. What does 'float' really mean?

Points of significant attainment to look for

Children:

- observe and describe events

- make simple predictions and compare what happened with what they expected

- respond to suggestions and put forward their own ideas to find answers to questions

- offer a variety of simple explanations for what happened

- sort materials on the basis of their properties

- explain why some materials are particularly suitable for specific purposes (wood for and in boats)

- know that water can oppose the downwards force of certain objects or materials

- know how the density of objects can affect their ability to float in water.

Additional ideas and resources

- Recite: 'Water' in *Out and About* by Shirley Hughes. Walker Books.

    'Bobby Shaftoe's gone to sea' (traditional rhyme).

20. Toy sledges
QCA links: 1E, 2E

Introduction

Children are experiencing forces physically (e.g. balancing, jumping, throwing, sliding, rolling toy cars, etc.) long before they are able to understand forces in the scientific sense. However, simple experiments help children to focus on specific forces, learn what these are and begin to use scientific terminology meaningfully in relevant contexts. Key Stage 1 and younger children will learn to use the words 'push' and 'pull' in a meaningful way. More able children can be introduced to the vocabulary and concepts of force, friction, different masses/weights and gravity.

Activity

Starting point

Make toy sledges by collecting small cardboard boxes (e.g. matchboxes, small sweet boxes), reinforced with sticky tape if necessary, and fastening approximately 1 m of string to one of the short ends of the boxes. Prepare a number of modelling clay 'marbles' to act as weights/masses to attach to the string. Able children can standardise these 'marbles' into 10 g or 20 g lumps.

> **H&S:** Modelling clay is preferred as standard weights/masses might fall off and cause bruising.

Make and place a tiny figure (e.g. Duplo, Lego, clay) in the sledge.

Development

Place the sledge on the table top and hang the string over the table edge (see Figure 4.5). Ask the children to make suggestions as to how to make the sledge move (various suggestions are acceptable). Add one of the clay marbles to the end of the string and ask the children to predict what will happen. What about adding more marbles? Allow some free exploration then ask how the different sledges can be tested in a fair way (e.g. released at the same time, carrying the same number of passengers). Use a prepared recording sheet or encourage the children to design their own (e.g. recording the amount of clay added each time and the distance travelled). Repeat the investigation adding more passengers to the sledge.

(NB: The sledge will always stop when the clay reaches the floor. Let the children work this out and suggest reasons why, then try different lengths of string and surfaces at different heights.)

Figure 4.5 Box sledge with toy person

Conclusion

Draw or write an account of what took place.

Organisation

If there is enough table top space, work in twos or threes (social or ability groups) for the sledges, taking turns to release, add weights/masses, measure the distance travelled, and record the results. Make the sledge move three times under the same conditions, then compare the 'best' performances (as in athletics) or take the average of three readings (able children).

(NB: Agreement is needed about how to release the sledges and measure the distances.)

Questions to encourage thinking skills

- Did the sledge do what you expected? Why/why not?
- How many clay marbles does it take to make the toy sledge just begin to move?
- What happens if you add more clay?
- How did you make it fair for each sledge?
- What happens if the string is longer? shorter?
- Why do you think things fall down to the ground? (Optional: Do you think they 'fall' out in space?)
- How many ways can you think of to make the sledge stop?
- How can you prevent the people falling out of the sledge when it brakes?
- What would happen if the table top/sliding surface is higher up? lower down?
- What kind of surfaces are best for sliding or skiing? Why might that be?

Vocabulary

brake, direction, force, friction, gravity, grip, heavy, light, mass, push, pull, resist, rough, safety belt, smooth, speed, surface, time, weight

Units: centimetres per second (cm/s) metres per second (mps or m/s)

Extension and enrichment activities

- Try the sledges on different surfaces (e.g. cloth, sandpaper, kitchen foil, carpet).
- Repeat the investigation using toy cars rolling down a ramp. Use a commercial or DIY ramp (a short plank with beading nailed to it near one end, hooked over a chair or strut). Predict the behaviour of different toy cars down the ramp (cars should differ according to their size, wheels, weight, passengers). Measure the distances travelled on and beyond the ramp and compare this with time (measured with a stopwatch) taken for the journey (see Figure 4.6).
- Make bar charts (by hand or using ICT) comparing (a) distance travelled by the cars, and (b) length of time travelling.
- Some children could calculate the speed (distance divided by time) in centimetres per second (cm/s) or metres per second (mps or m/s).
- Construct rolling vehicles with cereal packets or shoe boxes. Pierce holes in the sides (exactly opposite each other) for dowelling axles. Add commercial wheels (plastic or wooden) that fit tightly onto the dowelling or prevent loss of wheels with washers or modelling clay on the end of the dowelling. Decorate for a grand parade or carnival.
- Write the instructions for 'How to make a car with wheels'.

Points of significant attainment to look for

Children:

- suggest ways of collecting data to answer questions
- make careful observations and measurements of length and mass (weight) using simple equipment

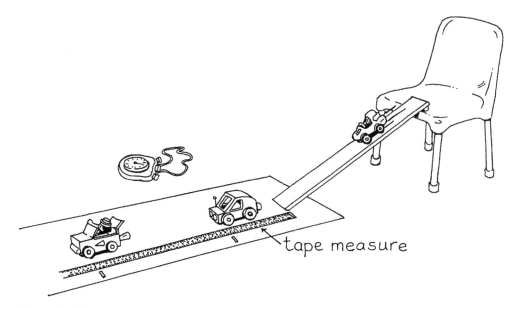

Figure 4.6 Toy cars on a ramp

- give explanations for what they observe happening
- record and communicate in a variety of ways what they found out
- suggest and carry out fair tests
- compare the movement of different objects in terms of distance, time taken and speed
- use knowledge of physical phenomena to link cause and effect (e.g. falling weights cause objects to fall to the ground/awareness that gravity is a force)
- generalise about slippery and rough surfaces (friction) in aiding or restricting movement
- use ICT to prepare and present results in graphical form.

Additional ideas and resources

- Read: *The Car Ride* by John Burningham. Walker Books.

  The Adventures of Little Wooden Horse by Ursula Moray Williams. Young Puffin.

  Bikes by Anne Rockwell. Picture Puffin.

- Sing: 'The wheels on the bus go round and round' in *Okki Tokki Unga* edited by B. Harrop. A & C Black.

21. Rockers and rollers!
QCA link: 2E

Introduction

As teachers we tend to spend more time on forces and motion than studying forces in equilibrium, which can be just as exciting. Young children are still glorying in their ability to balance – on low walls, PE apparatus, on tip-toe. Balancing toys are an excellent way of teaching a range of concepts about forces, including knowledge such as:

- forces act in different directions
- forces have different strengths
- forces have scientific names – push, pull, gravity
- forces can balance each other out so that they are in equilibrium
- all objects behave as if they have a centre of gravity or centre of mass.

Activity

Starting point

Prepare resources and some demonstration models in advance, such as a balancing clown (Figure 4.7 shows how to make one) and a balancing lemur

Figure 4.7 How to make a balancing clown

(see Figures 4.8 and 4.9). Demonstrate the models in sequential sessions or one by one in the initial discussion.

Development

Encourage the children to ask questions about them (any and all questions welcomed) and predict how they will behave. Ensure that the children have the resources to make individual models, then decorate and test them, recording results in a frame or table as shown in Table 4.1. Use the testing time to follow up the children's own questions and your own (see below). Use the plenary discussion to pool experiences and explanations.

Conclusion

Use a movement lesson in PE to create a clown movement where children are rocking clowns, made to rock back and forth with gentle pushers.

Organisation

Although children will be operating individually to make and test their models, group the children in friendship groups to help each other with ideas, manual support and positive feedback.

Questions to encourage thinking skills

Clown

- What do you think will happen if I push the clown to the left? Why do you think that?
- What happened? Why do you think that? Anything else?
- What can we do to make the clown lie down? Or? (i.e. use an additional downward force!)
- Do you think the clown could go on rocking for ever? Why not? (There is a friction force acting between the ping-pong ball and the table top, slowing it down.)

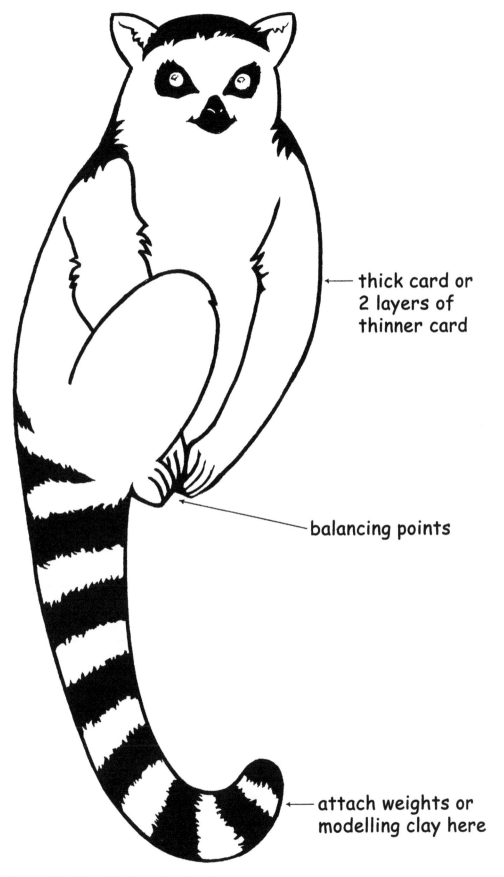

thick card or
2 layers of
thinner card

balancing points

attach weights or
modelling clay here

Figure 4.8 Template for balancing lemur

modelling clay
on lemur's tail

Figure 4.9 Using modelling clay to balance the lemur

Table 4.1 The effect of different masses of modelling clay on balancing toys

The clown
Draw or write what happens to the clown when you add different amounts of clay to the ping-pong ball.

Amount of modelling clay			
A little (5g)	**More (10g)**	**Even more (20g)**	**A lot (30g)**

The lemur
Draw or write what happens to the lemur when you add different amounts of clay to the lemur's tail. Now repeat putting different amounts of clay on its body.

		Amount of modelling clay			
		A little (5g)	**More (10g)**	**Even more (20g)**	**A lot (30g)**
Lemur's tail	top				
	middle				
	bottom				
Lemur's body	right				
	middle				
	left				

Balancing lemur

- How do you think I can make the lemur stay upright? (Try all suggestions – all involve a force.)
- What do you think will happen if I put the modelling clay in different places on its tail?
- What will happen if we put different weights on the body? Try.
- What do you think would happen in an aeroplane or a boat if it weren't balanced?

Vocabulary

above, balance, below, centre of gravity, centre of mass, different, direction, equal, equilibrium, gravity, heavier, heavy, less, light, lighter, mass, more, pull, push, same, uneven, weight

Units: grams (g)

Extension and enrichment activities

- Cut or saw an airflow ball in half and use a full-size lolly-stick clown. What is the minimum amount of modelling clay needed now to keep the clown stable and upright?
- Write instructions on 'How to make a rocking clown'.
- Write a story beginning either: 'Betty the bird couldn't balance. She . . .' or 'The rocking clown was tired. He wanted to lie down but every time he . . .'.
- Make some modelling clay animals, such as horses or cows, with only three stick legs. Test their balance. Encourage the children to think of animals with two legs, four legs, more legs. Which ones are best for balancing?
- Discuss 'Bungee jumpers' No. 11.1 in *Concept Cartoons in Science Education* by Stuart Naylor and Brenda Keogh (2000), as shown in Figure 4.10.

Points of significant attainment to look for

Children:

- explore and describe the way things move and balance
- carry out investigations to seek answers to questions about forces that balance each other
- make predictions about what will happen based on observations and experience
- record the effect of different weights/masses of modelling clay on the toys
- make comparisons and see patterns in movement and equilibrium
- talk about forces using scientific terms like 'push', 'pull' and 'balance' appropriately (and possibly 'gravity')

Figure 4.10 Bungee jumpers (Naylor and Keogh 2000)

- know that forces have different strengths ('a bigger push') and different directions ('it will bend down the other side')
- offer explanations/generalisations to others about why the toys move and balance ('when we push something it . . .', 'it won't balance unless we . . .').

Additional ideas and resources

- Describe all the things about clowns and other things that make us laugh.
- Sing: 'The Clown' in *Appusskidu* edited by B. Harrop. A & C Black.

22. Wind me up, Scotty!
QCA link: 1E

Introduction

Over 20 years ago, in a ground-breaking piece of research by the APU (the Assessment of Performance Unit, led by Professor Wynne Harlen), primary pupils' scientific skills were tested using, among other things, wind-up toys (Russell *et al.* 1988). The reasons for their use then are just as valid today – wind-up toys are fun, easy for younger children to investigate and are accurate enough to allow children to draw reasonable conclusions and create hypotheses.

Most wind-up or pull-back toys work on the principle of a coiled spring that stores energy which, when released, pushes a wheeled or 'walking' toy forwards. The distance the toy moves forward before it stops is dependent on how much energy is put in (i.e. how much it is wound up) and the friction between the wheels and the surface on which the toy moves.

It is worth buying a selection of 30 to 40 wind-up or pull-back toys for the school science resources as, although the initial cost may be a little expensive, only a few would need replacing each year.

Activity

Starting point
Collect a variety of wind-up or pull-back toys, whether wheeled vehicles or 'walking' toys. Before beginning any investigations, encourage the children to explore and play with the toys. This helps the children to refine their predictions. After the initial exploration, encourage the children to ask questions such as, 'How many things can we think of that have wheels? Anything else – maybe things that don't go on the road?' and to think of ways to compare them.

Development
Make sure that one of the tests will compare the number of wind-up turns with distance travelled, or distance pulled back compared with distance moved forward. Children who are measuring the length of time the toys move may need training in the use of a stopwatch first.

(NB: Remind the children that if we overwind a spring it can break, so testing to destruction may be interesting but not appropriate with these toys.)

Conclusion
Use the range of moving toys for a classroom display, with sets for regular sorting by the children.

Organisation

If you have enough toys for the whole class simultaneously, it is possible to have groups of four or five children, sorted by ability. Each group would need four or five toys to explore, predict and test.

Questions to encourage thinking skills

- What do you notice about the toys? Are any of them alike? In what way?

- How can we find out what they can do?

- How far do you think the toys will go with three/four/five full winds?

- How shall we measure the distance travelled? What if it travels in a curve instead of a straight line?

- How far forwards will the toys travel if we pull them back 10/20/30 cm (or two/three/four handspans)?

- What do you think is happening inside the toys when we wind them up? Could you draw what you think?

- How many winds do you think we need to make the toy go just exactly 30/40/50 cm (or handspans)?

- Why do you think the toys always stop moving?

- Which toy keeps moving for the longest time?

Vocabulary

backwards, better, compare, different, distance, energy, forward, friction, furthest, investigate, length, longer, longest, more, pull, push, question, release, same, spring, stop, surface, test, time, travel, wind

Units: length: (handspans) centimetres (cm) metres (m)
        time: seconds (s)

Extension and enrichment activities

- Use the data to construct a graph, by hand or using a compatible ICT program (see Useful Resources). Compare (a) the best or (b) the average of three tests. Interpret and explain the results.

- Carry out similar investigations with a variety of balls: airflow, tennis, squash, golf, baby's ball, etc. Encourage the children to think of their own questions and investigations, such as rolling, bouncing, bouncing on different surfaces, squeezing. Tests can be more controlled if the balls are rolled down a ramp and dropped from a given height. Although the tests cannot be purely scientific (the balls vary in too many ways: size, texture, material), the investigations can give very satisfactory results for this age group.

> **H&S:** Always ensure that the immediate drop area is clear to avoid the balls inadvertently hitting the children.

- Discuss 'Wind up' No. 15.1 in *Concept Cartoons in Science Education* by Stuart Naylor and Brenda Keogh (2000), as shown in Figure 4.11.

- Write poems about the noises that vehicles make on the road.

Figure 4.11 Wind up (Naylor and Keogh 2000)

Points of significant attainment to look for

Children:

– ask questions about the toys and decide how to find answers

– make predictions about their movement based on existing knowledge and first-hand experience

– estimate and measure distances travelled using non-standard or standard units

– consider the evidence of the way the toys move and draw conclusions

– use scientific terminology, such as 'push', 'pull', 'further' in a meaningful way

– recognise that when things move and travel, there is a cause and effect

– offer explanations to others about the way things move

– be aware that when objects move, there is an opposing force called 'friction'.

Additional ideas and resources

- Read: *The Big Red Bus Ride* by Peter Curry. Picture Lions.

  Little Blue Car by Gwen Grant and Susan Hellard. Orchard Books.

  The Adventures of Little Wooden Horse by Ursula Moray Williams. Young Puffin.

  Bikes by Anne Rockwell. Picture Puffin.

- Recite: 'The engineer' in *Now We Are Six* by A. A. Milne. Methuen.

- Sing: 'The wheels on the bus' in *Okki Tokki Unga* edited by B. Harrop. A & C Black.

23. Fallers and fliers
QCA links: 1E, 2E

Introduction

Children like to drop and throw things – sticks in the stream, balls in the air and flat stones across the water. What is exciting is that *something happens* – sticks travel down the stream, balls climb in the air then come down and bounce, stones bounce on the sea surface before sinking. All these demonstrate forces at work: gravity, water pressure, air friction. Objects dropped on Earth will accelerate towards the ground (gravity) but this can be slowed down or stopped by opposing forces, such as catching a ball before it hits the ground or by air friction. All objects in the absence of air will hit the ground at the same time. A feather will fall more slowly than a stone – the surface area of the feather and the downy gaps increase the amount of air friction. Parachutes and autogyros work on the latter principle by having a wide surface area relative to their overall mass.

Activity

Starting point

Introduce the activity to younger children by giving each child a supermarket bag tied to a piece of string to 'catch the air in it'. By running across the playground, children discover that the bag fills with air and exerts an opposing force to their running forwards. Very young children might stop here.

With older children, give each child a lump of modelling clay and allow them to drop it from a safe height. Discuss what happens (the clay falls quickly and is deformed on impact). Encourage the children to think what might happen if the modelling clay were a person and how we might slow down their fall if they were falling from an aircraft.

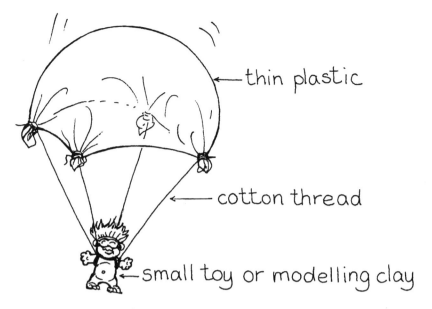

thin plastic

cotton thread

small toy or modelling clay

Figure 4.12 Making a parachute

Development

Cut pieces from thin plastic bags about 10 cm × 10 cm (round or square). Fasten equal lengths of cotton thread to the four 'corners' and tie them together at the bottom and add a small lump of modelling clay or stick to a small plastic toy person, e.g. Lego or Duplo (see Figure 4.12). Explore what happens now when this is dropped from a safe height before beginning any measured tests.

Test the parachutes with different amounts of clay or additional 'people' and discuss the 'best' performance. Try indoors and outdoors. More able children could time the drops using a stopwatch (needs training) and take the average of the best of each 3 drops to make a simple graph.

Conclusion

Give the children a recording frame so they can draw or write down their results (e.g. as shown in Table 4.2).

Organisation

Work in ability groups of threes so children can help each other with manual support, observation and timing.

Table 4.2 The effect of adding different amounts of modelling clay to the parachute

Draw or write what happened				
	Amount of modelling clay added to parachute			
Drop number	None	One lump (10g)	Two lumps (20g)	Three lumps (30g)
1				
2				
3				

Figure 4.13 Making an autogyro

Questions to encourage thinking skills

- What do you think makes things fall to the ground?
- How many different ways can we think of to slow down the modelling clay?
- What happened when we tied a parachute to the clay? Why do you think that?
- What will happen if we add more clay? make the parachute bigger? make the cotton threads shorter? longer?
- What will happen if we drop the parachutes outside?
- What happened outside? Why do you think that? Could it be anything else?

Vocabulary

air, air resistance, area, bigger, direction, distance, force, friction, gravity, heavier, height, length, lighter, mass, speed, surface, time, weight

Units: length: centimetres (cm) metres (m)   time: seconds (s)

Extension and enrichment activities

- Try different sizes of parachute and different shapes, perhaps different thicknesses.
- Make simple autogyros (Figure 4.13) and test them with one/two/three small paper clips. Make larger ones and test again.
- Create a movement in PE based on things falling and flying. Demonstrate in Sharing Assembly.
- Make up an imaginary graph of 'The adventures of the red umbrella' using time (o'clock) on the *x* axis and height on the *y* axis, using either standard units (metres) or non-standard units (head height, trees, houses, birds flying, etc.) (see Figure 4.14).

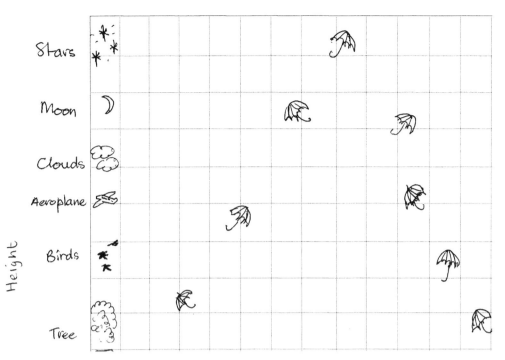

Figure 4.14 The adventures of the red umbrella

- Use a digital or ordinary camera to photograph the children flying their kites and use for a classroom or corridor display.
- Discuss 'Falling' No.11.2 in *Concept Cartoons in Science Education* by Stuart Naylor and Brenda Keogh (2000), as shown in Figure 4.15.

Figure 4.15 Falling (Naylor and Keogh 2000)

Points of significant attainment to look for

Children:

– explore the way things fall, ask questions and decide how to find answers

– help to plan investigations on parachutes

– record observations and simple measurements of time or distance in a table

– compare the effect of different masses of modelling clay on the parachutes and identify patterns in the behaviour

– explain what they did to others and offer simple explanations for the results

– use scientific terminology, such as 'area', 'heavier', 'gravity', 'air resistance/friction' in a meaningful way.

Additional ideas and resources

● For a special display or parents' evening, set up a hair drier on a cool setting with the nozzle pointing vertically upwards, position a ping-pong ball above this and switch on. The Bernoulli effect on both sides of the ball prevents the ball from rising or falling – the forces are in balance.

● Recite: 'Hey diddle, diddle, the cat and the fiddle' (traditional rhyme).

'There was an old woman tossed up in a basket' (traditional rhyme).

'Jack and Jill' (traditional rhyme).

24. Who's that crossing *my* bridge?
QCA links: 1C, 3C

Introduction

Bridges in the UK offer some of the finest examples of structures in the built environment and represent how we use materials and forces and technology to provide solutions to our needs, such as crossing a river, valley or motorway. We could include tunnels and subways in this group of structures also. We have road, rail and pedestrian bridges, bridges over canals, and in airports where runways straddle other working spaces.

Bridges are usually one of three types:

● slab bridges (vertical supports and horizontal causeway – for short spans between supports and mostly used in ancient bridges such as stone bridges and Roman aqueducts)

● arch bridges (the arch transfers the compression forces along the arch – again, for shorter spans)

● suspension bridges (the flat horizontal is supported by wires/cables which counteract the compression forces and they, in turn, are supported by ground-based cables providing the tension).

Activity

Starting point

If there is a bridge (road, rail, canal, pedestrian) that you and the children can visit safely, arrange to see it. With or without a visit, create a river or motorway in the classroom with blue or brown crêpe paper, varying from 20 to 40 cm wide. Discuss what bridges are for and what they look like.

Development

Children use one or more of the following materials to design and make free-standing bridges across the river/road:

1. construction bricks – both interlocking and non-interlocking. Test the strength using toy cars or toy pedestrians
2. found materials, gluesticks and sticky tape
3. newspaper and sticky tape only
4. (for able children) art straws, pipe cleaners and sticky tape.

(NB: If children have difficulty, it is better to bend the rules so that they succeed. They will still learn from what did not work.)

Conclusion

Take photographs of the bridges and the children. Display these with written accounts from the able children describing the problems in building they had and the solutions they found.

Organisation

Work in ability groups of four children allowing each group either a free choice of materials or giving each group materials commensurate with their skills and a span to match. Photograph the bridges as soon as they are built and before they are tested as some may collapse.

Questions to encourage thinking skills

- What do you think will be the most difficult part of the bridge building? Why do you think that?
- Why have you chosen to use those materials? Why did you decide to do it that way?
- Why do you think your bridge works so well?
- What could we do to make your bridge stronger?
- What would have made it easier to build your bridge?
- What do you think are the weakest parts of your bridge? Why do you think that?

Vocabulary

bridge, build, construct, distance, far, gravity, length, long, material ,short, span, stable, strength, strong, support, weak, width

Units: centimetres (cm)   grams (g)

Extension and enrichment activities

- Make a free-standing bridge to cross the widest part of the river/road to support five, ten or more cars.

- Use found materials or construction bricks to construct a tunnel with a roof height big enough to take a large wheeled toy or something similar.

- Research different kinds of bridges in books, CD-ROMs and on the Internet.

- Create an individual or class book on bridges in the locality, the UK or around the world: Forth, Cardiff, Newcastle upon Tyne, London Millennium, Sydney Harbour, San Francisco.

- In PE, alone and with partners, develop movements to create bridge shapes to span spaces, using legs, arms, ribbons and ropes, etc.

Points of significant attainment to look for

Children:

- respond to suggestions and put forward their own ideas to solve problems
- explore the properties of materials
- co-operate with others
- explain what they did to others and offer simple explanations for the results
- know about forces and equilibrium and use strategies to create stable structures
- use scientific terminology, such as 'force', 'gravity', 'span', 'strong', 'support', 'weak', in a meaningful way.

Additional ideas and resources

- Decorate the bridges for a real or pretend festival.
- Tell the story of 'Goldilocks and the three bears'. Some children could design a chair that only collapses when a toy bear sits on it.
- Read: *The Three Billy Goats Gruff*. Ladybird Easy Reading Books.

    The Three Little Pigs and the Big Bad Wolf. Ladybird Easy Reading Books.

- Sing: 'London Bridge is falling down' (traditional rhyme – discuss the houses on it, why the fire of London could so easily burn down so many houses, etc.).

25. Colour and camouflage
QCA links: 1D, 2B, 3F

Introduction

Colour is not listed as a statutory learning objective for five- to seven-year-old children. It is true that the understanding of different wavelengths of light is not appropriate for this age group, but knowledge of colour certainly is, and even nursery children can describe and differentiate between colours and begin to understand the nature of colour in the environment.

Visible light is composed of several colours (as originally defined by Newton): red, orange, yellow, green, blue, indigo, violet (ROYGBIV). When light meets an object all the light may be reflected (as in mirrors) or only some of that light (as in coloured objects). What we see as colour are the wavelengths of light that are reflected: red when everything but red is absorbed, black when all colours are absorbed. Most plants look green because they are so efficient they absorb most of the light energy except green.

Thin films and angled glass (bubbles, oil on the road, a rainbow, and prisms) can split 'white' light into its separate colour wavelengths. In the environment, colour is used by living things to attract and repel.

Activity A: Bubbles

Make a bubble solution by mixing approximately one part good washing-up liquid to five parts tap water. Use blowers made from florists' wire twisted into loops and different shapes and giant blowers made from cut-down washing-up bottle tops, with fringes (see Figure 14.16). Dip the blowers into the solution without stirring and blow gently but firmly to create bubbles.

> **H&S:** Take care not to blow or burst bubbles in people's faces.

Activity B: Camouflage

Visit a nearby garden and look at the colours found there, especially the colours of the plants and small creatures if you see any. Discuss reasons why we might not easily see animals among the leaves or the undergrowth.

Use paint, crayons or felt-tip pens to colour and cut out real or make-believe garden bugs. Take the cut-out bugs into an area of growing plants. Predict which animals will be easily camouflaged among the plants. Investigate the predictions in different places. Then redesign some bugs using colours to make them very camouflaged on one side (e.g. on tree bark, among green leaves, under

cut down plastic washing up liquid bottle – with 'fringe'

bubble solution – don't whisk!

Figure 4.16 Creating bubbles

brown leaf mould, etc.). The other side can be very colourful to attract mates. Test again.

Conclusion

Display the children's garden bugs against different coloured paper backgrounds or on bubble prints (see Extension and enrichment activities) with a question: 'Which colour is best for hiding?'

Questions to encourage thinking skills

- How many different colours can you see in the bubbles?
- Can you see any reflections? Which way up are they?
- Where else might you see different colours like these?
- What is your favourite colour? Why is that?
- How can we find out which is the most favourite colour in the class?
- What colours do *we* use to inform us about: danger? people at work? traffic lights?
- Why do some animals hide? (e.g. hiding from predators)
- Why do some animals want to be seen? (e.g. poisonous/to attract mates, etc.)
- Which are the best colours to be camouflaged against the soil? among leaves? in a rock pool? under water?

Vocabulary

absorb, attract, camouflage, colour, danger, environment, film, frighten, light, predator, prey, reflect, solution, wavelength (if appropropriate: carbon dioxide, chlorophyll, oxygen, photosynthesis, water)

Units: millilitres (ml)

Extension and enrichment activities

- Write a story: 'One day I blew a bubble so big I fell inside it. I was in Rainbow Land! It was . . .'.
- Make bubble prints. Mix some washing-up liquid into thick paints. Pour separate colours into saucers. Use straws to blow bubbles into the paint. Gently lie a piece of white paper over the bubbles and allow to settle.
- Use musical instruments to illustrate rainbow colours, sea and sky colours, etc.
- (For able children) Use coloured filters and test these by looking at a range of different coloured objects. Explain or record what they *can* see and what they *can't* see, e.g.:

Red object   Orange   Yellow   Green   etc.

    e.g. Through the red filter the red brick looks . . ., the green one looks . . .

- Use books, websites and other resources to research animals and their colours, including the chameleon and others. More able children can focus on a particular animal and draw and write about it and its habitat.

Points of significant attainment to look for

Children:

- observe, explore and describe features of objects, living things and events
- ask questions and investigate to seek answers to these questions
- make predictions and offer explanations for phenomena
- use appropriate scientific language
- know that living things are adapted to their environment
- know that white light consists of other wavelengths of coloured light.

Additional ideas and resources

- Cut out a set of coloured cards and insert in the front of reading books as critical reviews, for example: Green = Great! Yellow = Quite good, Red = Not so good.
- Read: *Mouse Paint* by Ellen Stoll Walsh. Orchard Books.

             Mr Rabbit and the Lovely Present by C. Zolotow and M. Sendak. Picture Puffin.
- Recite: 'The slippery soap song' in *Bedtime Rhymes*. John Foster and Carol Thompson. Oxford University Press.
- Sing: 'Sing a rainbow' in *Apusskidu*. A & C Black.

             'Ten green bottles' (traditional rhyme).

26. Me and my shadow
QCA links: 1D, 3F

Introduction

We see when there is light – with no light, we cannot see. Shadows are formed when light rays meet an opaque object. Light travels in straight lines. Young children are usually fascinated by shadows, especially their own. It is not always easy for children to link cause and effect with their shadows and our very distant, very small sun. It can take repeated experiences for them to know this and understanding may come later. If possible, initiate this investigation by inviting children into a darkened classroom in the daytime (shutters or blinds closed). Pretend to have difficulty reading the Register until the children suggest putting on the light or opening the blinds, explaining we need light to see.

Activity

Starting points

Start outside on a sunny day, looking at and discussing the children's shadows and what is happening to make these (light cannot bend around objects or pass through most materials so if we stand in the way of the sun's rays we block out the light and create a shadow).

In the classroom, hang a small sheet or white tablecloth so that it forms a screen just touching the floor. Angle a table lamp with strong watt bulb (say, 100 w) so that light falls onto the screen. Choose one child (A) to stand behind the lamp and one child (B) to stand between the lamp and the screen. Before the lamp is switched on, invite the children to predict which child, (A) or (B), will create a shadow on the screen and why.

Development

Test the children's ideas, asking some of the questions to encourage thinking skills, and confirm by testing with other children. Introduce other objects and invite predictions as to the type of shadows they will produce: book, toy, handlens, clear plastic bag, lunch box, pencil, glass jar.

Conclusion

Use a movement lesson in PE to play shadows, with each child having his or her own 'shadow child'. A further challenge is added by requiring the shadows to always stay on the same side, opposite the light source!

Organisation

Begin and develop the activity as a whole class. Divide into small groups to do repeat tests of shadow and objects.

Questions to encourage thinking skills

- Which person do you think will cast a shadow, A or B?
- What do you think will happen to our shadows if I move the lamp higher? lower?
- Can you predict where you think the shadow will be?
- Can you think of a way to make our shadows bigger without moving the lamp?
- What type of shadow do you think the book will make? the glass jar? Why do you think that?
- Why do you think some things make a 'better' shadow than others?
- Can you think of a way to use our shadow outside to tell the time?

Vocabulary

block, dark, darkness, light, opaque, shadow, silhouette, transparent

Units: time o'clock

Extension and enrichment activities

- Use the lamp behind the screen with the audience in front for a shadow puppet play using toy people and animals.
- Use the back-lit screen and audience for a guessing game. Provide a collection of objects and shapes and present them so that the shadow silhouettes are less obvious: a book or toy on edge to the light, a ruler from its end or side, a cylinder from the end.
- Invite suggestions about the possible adventures of 'The Shadow who ran away'. Write or dramatise these.
- Discuss 'Shadow screen' No. 12.2 in *Concept Cartoons in Science Education* by Stuart Naylor and Brenda Keogh (2000), as shown in Figure 2.2.

Points of significant attainment to look for

Children:

- think of ways to answer questions
- predict/think about what will happen when objects block the light
- carry out simple investigations
- offer explanations about what is happening when light meets opaque/transparent objects
- know that darkness is the absence of light
- know that we cannot see when there is no light
- know that light cannot pass through some materials and this leads to the formation of shadows.

Additional ideas and resources

- Pin or stick black sugar paper to the screen or a wall. Use the lamp to cast a head silhouette, draw round with chalk and cut out. Use for an identification game and display.
- Read: *Peter Pan* by J. M. Barrie. Puffin Classics.

  The Very Lonely Firefly by Eric Carle. Hamish Hamilton.

  The Owl who was Afraid of the Dark by Jill Tomlinson. Young Puffin.
- Recite: 'In the dark' in *Now We Are Six* by A. A. Milne. Methuen.

---

27. Mirror, mirror on the wall!
QCA link: 1D

Introduction

Before the silvered glass mirrors we use today, people looked at their reflection in water, or shiny metal surfaces such as polished bronze that were only available to the rich. Clear water or shiny surfaces reflect back more of the light falling on their surface than dull materials. Rays of light are reflected rather like a ball bouncing on a wall: thrown at right angles, the ball comes straight back, thrown from one side, the ball bounces off to the other side. Light behaves in the same way and in the process, the image is reversed – we see our right eye on the left of the mirror image – but this reversal concept is less relevant to younger children's learning.

Children need good quality plane mirrors to explore reflection, preferably flexible ones. Scratched or dull mirrors should be replaced – old plastic mirrors can be used for other purposes (see Extension and enrichment activities).

Activity

Starting point
Use individual (preferably plastic) plane mirrors for children to observe themselves. Ask the children to describe everything they can see.

Development
Encourage the children to explore how they can use mirrors to see behind them, sideways or round corners. Finally, flex the mirrors into concave and convex shapes to discover the kind of images produced in curved mirrors.

Conclusion
Children draw their mirror reflections. Able children could try to draw funny faces that when held up to a curved mirror appear normal.

Organisation

With enough mirrors, children could complete individual exploration then work in small groups or in pairs to support each other's exploration of seeing things behind them or round corners.

Questions to encourage thinking skills

- What can you see in the mirror? Can we see ourselves in wood? paper?
- How many materials can you find in which you can see your own reflection? What do you notice about all these materials?
- Do you think we can see our reflections in the dark? How could we find out?
- Where do you have to put the mirror or your eyes so without turning round, you can see the classroom door? the window? the book corner?
- What happens to your reflection when the mirror curves inwards (concave) or outwards (convex)?
- What kind of funy face drawn on paper would look normal in a curved mirror?

Vocabulary

angle, bend, concave, convex, curved, dark, light, plane, reflect, reflection, shiny, surface

Extension and enrichment activities

- Use masking tape to fasten two plastic mirrors together. Cut up or use prepared fragments of shiny paper/stars/tiny buttons (from haberdashers) and put a few in between the two mirrors. Look and then move these around. Alternatively, do this with commercial kaleidoscopes. Encourage children to describe, draw or paint some of the patterns they see.
- Use the diagram shown in Figure 4.17 to cut out and glue together the cardboard periscope (see Figure 4.18). Use square pieces of plastic mirror and glue in position as shown, then fold inwards at 45° angles. Use to see over obstacles and around corners.
- Write instructions for visitors to a submarine: 'Why we need a periscope when we are below the sea.'
- Write a story: 'I found a magic mirror. When I looked inside it . . .'.
- Make a display of objects and materials with reflective/shiny surfaces.

Points of significant attainment to look for

Children:

- explore reflective surfaces using first-hand experience
- respond to questions about vision by trying to find answers
- compare materials on the basis of their properties (shiny/dull)
- know that light is reflected from some surfaces and not from others

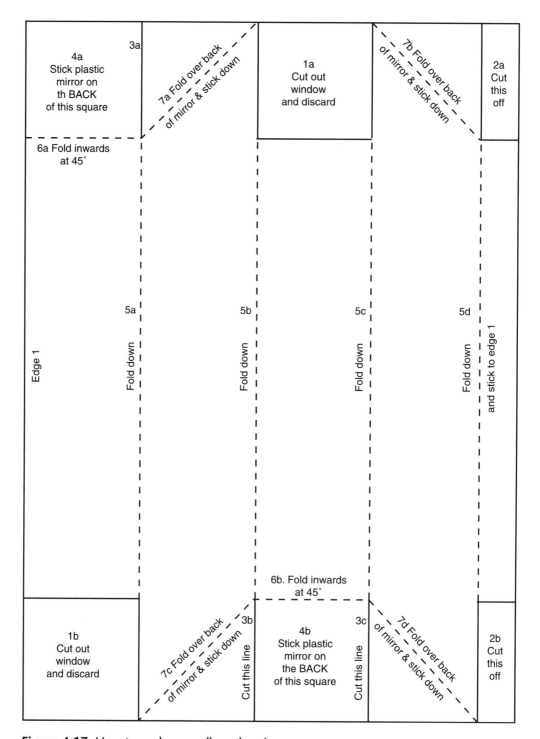

Figure 4.17 How to make a cardboard periscope

- know that we cannot see when there is no light/darkness is the absence of light
- offer explanations to others about what they think is happening.

Additional ideas and resources

- Use wet paint or acrylics to make fold paintings – mirror image prints.
- Dramatise the story of *Snow White and the Seven Dwarves* (Benwig Books) from the point of view of the magic mirror.

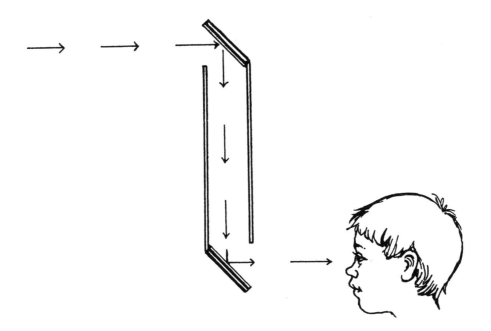

Figure 4.18 A cardboard periscope

28. Noisy vibrations!
QCA link: 1F

Introduction

Sound is made by vibrating materials – whether metal, wood, rubber, water or air. A vacuum does not transmit any sound. Sound vibrations occur in waves with areas of compression and rarefaction analogous to water waves with peaks and troughs. Loud sounds occur when the materials vibrate with great energy, quieter sounds with less energy. Pitch is determined by the frequency of the waves per second. The greater the frequency, or the more vibrations per second, the higher the note. We measure volume of sound in decibels and frequency in Herz (also written as Hz). Musical notes range in pitch from 30 to 3,000 Hz, or 30 to 3,000 vibrations per second. Middle C on the piano is 256 Hz, or 256 vibrations per second.

Human ears have an upper limit of about 18,000 Hz (though this decreases with age), dogs and cats about 30,000 Hz, and bats about 100,000 Hz.

Activity A: What is making this sound?

Starting point
Assemble a variety of different opaque containers (e.g. tins, plastic pots) with items inside, such as grains of rice, grains of sand, full of sand, cotton wool, keys, plastic counters, large beans, marbles, coins. Have ready some additional empty containers and items, such as a wooden brick, salt, conkers, leaves, a mitten, toy car.

Development

Play a guessing game by shaking the containers and asking the children to predict what they contain, then open and show. Invite the children to predict what sounds the additional items will make and why. Test these.

Conclusion

Encourage the children to explain how they think we hear and either draw a picture of their ideas and/or draw a partner's ear.

Activity B: Vibrations

Explore vibrations by demonstrating and encouraging explanations for the following:

1. Rap a tuning fork on a hard, cloth-covered surface then immediately touch the surface of a dish of water – the water vibrates and splashes!

2. Put a few grains of rice on a drum skin and strike the drum from below or at the side – the rice grains jump as the drum skin vibrates!

3. Pluck a guitar or violin string then stop the sound with a touch of the hand.

4. Play some notes on a recorder, trumpet or coconut shells and invite the children to explain what might be vibrating inside each of these instruments.

Questions to encourage thinking skills

- What do you think is inside making that sound? What makes you think that?
- Why do you think the tin full of . . . doesn't make much noise?
- What sounds do you think these objects will make? Why do you think that?
- Why do you think we need to protect our ears from very loud sounds?
- What do I have to do to make a sound with the tuning fork? drum? guitar?
- What is making the rice grains jump? the water splash?
- What do you think is moving inside the recorder?

Vocabulary

high, higher, loud, louder, low, lower, move, noise, pitch, quiet, sound, vibrate, vibrations, volume

Units: volume/loudness of sound: decibels (dB)

Extension and enrichment activities

- Make DIY string instruments with shoe boxes, or similar, and elastic bands. Have a variety of boxes and various thicknesses and lengths of elastic bands. Test for different sounds.

> **H&S:** Remind the children not to play these too near the face as occasionally an elastic band will wear and snap.

- Record different sounds on a tape and put it in a tape recorder with ear phones for the children to listen to and guess the sources. Discuss their ideas in a plenary.
- Research secondary sources of information to find out how cats and dogs hear, and how bats use hearing to find their prey. Make a presentation of the findings or use for a class book on 'Animal Ears' to which other children can add further information.

Points of significant attainment to look for

Children:

– explore materials that make sounds

– explore different sources of sound

– make simple comparisons and identify patterns and associations

– offer explanations for observations based on first-hand experience

– know that we hear sounds through our ears

– know that when objects vibrate they can make sounds

– know that there are different kinds of sound and different sources of sound

– know that sounds can be louder and quieter, higher and lower.

Additional ideas and resources

- Use the containers with items and/or instruments to create the sound effects for a rhyme, story or song (e.g. 'Jack and the beanstalk'/'London Bridge is falling down').
- Read: *Little Beaver and The Echo* by Amy MacDonald and Sarah Fox-Davies. Walker Books.

   The Musicians of Bremen (traditional). Benwig Books.
- Sing: 'Sing a song of sixpence' (traditional rhyme).

29.   The weather forecast
QCA link: 3D

Introduction

Why study weather? Everyday we experience the weather, although sometimes it is more dramatic than usual or more investigable. Our behaviour is influenced by it and so are crop growth and harvests, and with the climate changing, children need to develop awareness and responsibility towards their environment.

Space is limited here so we have concentrated on rain and wind. Rainfall occurs when water evaporates to form clouds, and when those clouds come to an area of different pressure they release the water as rain. Winds are generated by differentials in air temperatures and by the revolution of the Earth, and a combination of the two.

Activities A: Rain

- Collect rain in a narrow jar with a wide funnel on top and measure and record the amount collected each day over a period of a week or two. The jar can be calibrated and a drop of food colouring in the bottom can make it easier for young children to read. (NB: Although this is not a strictly accurate method of measuring daily rainfall it enables younger children to make the measurements, as sometimes differences between small daily amounts, such as 2 ml or 4 ml, are difficult for them to read.)

- Explore raincoats and other waterproof clothing and test these with water poured from a small watering can (see Figure 4.19). Compare other fabrics and test for water absorbency.

- Make raindrops on fingers: dip hands into water and allow to drip. Discuss the shape of the drops and how they fall, etc.

- Make a raincloud in the classroom using grey cloth or paper on the ceiling and cotton threads hanging down, each one with raindrops attached cut from transparent acetate.

- Research deserts and rain forests and use creative materials to turn a nearby corridor into a rain forest.

Figure 4.19 How waterproof are these fabrics?

Figure 4.20 Windy day (Naylor and Keogh 2000)

Activities B: Wind

- If possible, buy a wind vane (from an educational supplier or garden centre), position it in a safe, open place and observe the direction of the wind and any changes or gusts. For younger children estimate wind strength with a long ribbon tied to a stick.

- Fasten inflated balloons or plastic bags or one leg of a pair of tights to strings. Hold them up in the wind and discuss what happens. Discuss the use of wind socks at airports (aircraft tend to take off and land into the wind).

- Watch the weather reports on TV and design weather symbols for a class weather chart. More able children could look up international symbols on the Met Office website (www.metoffice.com) and the website for BBC TV weather forecasts (www.bbc.co.uk/weather).
- Write a story about 'The Wind who lost its blow!'

Questions to encourage thinking skills

Rain:

- What does rainwater look like? rain drops?
- Where does the rain come from? How do you think the water gets into the clouds? (Accept all answers, only discuss the water cycle if appropriate.)
- What might happen if we got no rain? too much rain?
- What are places called where there is no rain? lots of rain?

Wind:

- What is making the balloon, bag or wind vane move?
- Where is the wind coming from? What makes you think that?
- What do you think the wind is made of?
- What might happen if we had too much wind? no wind at all?

Vocabulary

absorb, absorbent, cloud, cold, forecast, heat, hot, rain, shade, snow, sunlight, waterproof, weather, wind, wind vane

Units: temperature: degrees Celsius (°C)

Points of significant attainment to look for

Children:

- explore aspects of the weather, make observations and collect data
- carry out investigations to find answers to questions
- make simple comparisons and see patterns
- know about changes in the weather and the environment
- are aware of the effect of weather conditions on how we live.

Additional ideas and resources

- Discuss 'Windy Day' No.13.9 in *Concept Cartoons in Science Education* by Stuart Naylor and Brenda Keogh (2000), as shown in Figure 4.20.
- Read: *The Wind Blew* by Pat Hutchins. Red Fox Picture Books.

    What's the Weather? by Maureen Roffey. Macmillan.
- Recite: 'Happiness' in *When We Were Very Young* by A. A. Milne. Methuen.
- Sing: 'I love the Sun' in *Someone's Singing, Lord.* A & C Black.

Tables of Significant Attainment

Table 1: Progression of Significant Attainment

Life processes and living things – Plants as living organisms

Scientific enquiry skills and attitudes, ICT skills

Context

- Identify differences between living things and things that have never lived.
- Plants have basic life processes, e.g. they grow, change, respond to their environment.
- Different parts of plants have a specific name and function.

Concepts

- Plants are different from non-living things because they: get bigger by growing, produce food for growth, move and respond to changes or stimuli from the environment, produce new, living things similar to them by reproduction.
- Plants are organised into special parts which carry out the processes of life.

Vocabulary and Système International (SI) units

air, autumn, bark, conditions, environment, flower, food, germinate, grow, healthy, leaf, light, natural, petal, plant, pollen, produce, reproduce, roots, seeds, spring, stem, summer, survive, temperature, tree, warmth, water, winter

Length: centimetre (cm) metre (m)   Mass: kilogram (kg) gram (g)

Time: second (s, sec) minute (min)   Temperature: degrees Celsius (°C)

Volume: litres (l) millilitre (ml)

Progression of Learning Outcomes

Children know that:

Plants are different from animals. There are different sorts of plants.

Plants have an external structure and each part has a special name – leaf, flower, stem and root.

Children are able to:

Describe simply the similarities and differences between plants and leaves.

Describe simply how plants change as they grow (e.g. girth, height, roots, etc.).

Describe the growth of living things by talk and record changes by drawing pictures/charts of different results.

Explore sources of information, including ICT, and talk about what they found out.

Work co-operatively.

Children know that:

Plants:

- grow,
- reproduce new living plants, and
- need food, water, air and warmth.

Plants can be sorted by different criteria (leaves, fruit, flowers, etc.)

Different plants grow in different places.

Plants need particular conditions to survive (light, water, warmth).

Children are able to:

Ask and respond to questions and with help, seek answers to these questions.

In observations describe key factors helping plants stay alive.

Make comparisons of size and colour of plants, stems, leaves or roots.

Measure and compare length and height using non-standard measurements, and record them in prepared charts.

Offer simple predictions for what might happen in an investigation of growing plants.

Offer explanations for their observations and for simple patterns in recorded data (e.g. seed growth in the dark compared with growth in the light).

Begin to organise and classify information using ICT and present their findings.

Enter, save and retrieve work.

Share ideas and co-operate with others.

Children know that:

Plants need the right conditions to be healthy and grow by describing how to care for a plant.

The different parts of plants have particular functions: roots, leaves, stem, flower, seeds.

Living plants can die and decay (e.g. from age, drought, flooding, bacteria).

Living things are different from non-living things.

Certain types of human behaviour and natural phenomena can improve or harm the natural environment.

Children are able to:

Ask questions, respond to suggestions and with help, seek answers to these questions, e.g. growing seeds in the dark or the light.

Make simple predictions about the growth of a plant.

Make simple SI measurements of length, height and mass, enter results in tables and write about them.

Interpret and explain the patterns they observe in results and investigations.

Use simple scientific vocabulary in a meaningful context.

Use ICT to save information and to find and use appropriate stored information.

Use ICT to generate, develop, organise and present their work.

Co-operate with others.

Begin to organise and classify information using ICT and present their findings.

Show an open-minded attitude to other people's ideas.

Children know that:

Leaves have an important function in the life process of the plant and they need light to carry out this process.

Seeds and roots absorb water as part of the life process.

There are different seeds and they germinate to produce plants similar to the parent plant.

Human behaviour and other natural factors can improve or harm the natural environment.

A good human diet needs to include different edible plants as a source of vitamins and minerals.

Children are able to:

Plan and carry out an investigation using an approach that is as fair as possible (fair testing).

Use scientific equipment safely and appropriately. *cont.*

Make a series of observations and measurements in seeking answers to questions, e.g. changes in growth.

Offer predictions based on prior experience and observations.

Plot simple graphs and interpret patterns in the data.

Offer explanations for perceived patterns, using scientific language as appropriate (e.g. plants in conditions of warmth, water and light grow better than in other conditions).

Suggest reasons for and ways of improving their work.

Use a variety of sources, including ICT, to seek information.

Use ICT in a variety of ways to record and present information to an audience.

Begin to use sensors to collect physical data (e.g. light, temperature).

Show a reflective, open-minded attitude to themselves and others.

Table 2: Progression of Significant Attainment

Humans and other animals

Scientific enquiry skills and attitudes, ICT skills

Context

- Identify differences between living things and things that have never lived.
- Humans are a kind of animal.
- Animals have basic life processes.
- Different parts of animals have a specific name and function.
- Consider the life processes of nutrition, movement, growth and reproduction.
- Consider the need for hygiene and diet for good health.

Concepts

- Animals are different from non-living things because they: get bigger by growing, produce food for nutrition and growth, move and respond to changes or stimuli from the environment, produce new, living things similar to them by reproduction.
- Animals are organised into special parts which carry out the processes of life.

Vocabulary and SI units

animal, backbone, blood, bones, breathe, circulate, conditions, consume, diet, excrete, food, muscles, natural, nutrition, offspring, pulse, reproduce, senses, skeleton, skin, stomach, survive, temperature, vitamin, water

Length: centimetre (cm) metre (m)   Mass: kilogram (kg) gram (g)

Temperature: degrees Celsius (°C)   Area: square cm (sq cm/cm²)

Progression of Learning Outcomes

Children know that:

There are different sorts of animals.

Animals have an external structure and each part has a special name – head, hand, foot, teeth, etc.

There are differences between sexes and ages of human beings.

Children are able to:

Describe simply how animals/humans change as they grow.

Describe the observed physical differences between different humans by talking or record by pictures/simple charts.

Explore sources of information, including ICT, and talk about this.

Work co-operatively.

Children know that:

Animals, including humans:

- grow, and
- reproduce new living animals.

Animals, including humans, need food, water, air and warmth.

Animals can be sorted into groups, using physical characteristics.

Different animals are found in different places.

Children are able to:

Describe key factors that help humans stay alive.

Make comparisons of size and different external parts of their bodies, like hands or feet.

Compare height and other features using non-standard measurements and record in prepared charts.

Make simple predictions about what they might observe.

Offer explanations for their observations and for simple patterns in recorded data.

Begin to organise and classify information using ICT and present their findings.

Enter, save and retrieve work.

Share ideas and co-operate with others.

Children know that:

Animals need the right conditions to be healthy and grow.

Food and a balanced diet are needed for activity, growth and health.

Different physical features are linked to function (e.g. hands for sensing, feet for balancing and other movement, skin, bone, muscles, nose, eyes).

Animals/humans have a life cycle.

Children are able to:

Ask questions, respond to suggestions and, with help, seek answers to these questions, e.g. comparing the area of the foot with the area of the shoe sole.

Make simple predictions about, say, the size of different fingers.

Make simple SI measurements of length, height and mass, enter results in tables and write about them.

Interpret and explain the patterns they observe in results and investigations.

Use simple scientific vocabulary in a meaningful context (e.g. average, similar).

Use ICT to save information and to find and use appropriate stored information.

Use ICT to generate, develop, organise and present their work.

Co-operate with others.

Show an open-minded attitude to other people's ideas.

Children know that:

Humans have internal and external organs and that these have particular functions.

There are observable changes in the human body associated with ageing.

Humans reproduce and produce living beings that can show characteristics of the parents.

A good balanced diet and hygiene is necessary for good health.

Children are able to:

Plan and carry out a scientific enquiry using an approach that is as fair as possible (e.g. comparing hand area, finger length).

Use scientific equipment safely and appropriately.

Make a series of observations and measurements in seeking answers to questions, e.g. comparison of individual finger prints.

Offer predictions based on prior experience and observations.

Offer explanations for perceived patterns, using scientific language as appropriate (e.g. area, trend).

Suggest reasons for and ways of improving their work. *cont.*

Use a variety of sources, including ICT, to seek information.

Use ICT in a variety of ways to record and present information to an audience.

Show a reflective, open-minded attitude to themselves and others (e.g. celebrating the things we share in common with other humans as well as individual differences).

Table 3: Progression of Significant Attainment

Life processes and living things – Variation and classification

Scientific enquiry skills and attitudes, ICT skills

Context

- Recognise similarities and differences between themselves and others.
- Learn to group living things using observable similarities and differences.
- Use observable features to group locally found living things and use a key for the purpose of identification.
- Use characteristic features to devise a simple key to help identify animals and plants belonging to a common group.

Concepts

- There is a wide variety of living things and these can be grouped by observable characteristics.
- Living things reproduce and some characteristics are inherited from one generation to the next.

Vocabulary and SI units

animal, autumn, backbone, bird, coat, conditions, egg, environment, fish, flower, group, inherit, insect, key, leaf, limbs, mammal, offspring, petal, plant, reproduce, root, seeds, skin, spring, stem, summer, tree

Progression of Learning Outcomes

Children know that:

There are some obvious physical differences between common plants and animals around them.

There is a variety of living things and they are different in appearance (e.g. bird, fish). *cont.*

Children are able to:

Describe simple similarities and differences between two common animals or plants (e.g. fish, and themselves or woodlice and snails).

Describe observed physical differences by talking or record by pictures/simple charts.

Explore sources of information, including ICT, and talk about this.

Work co-operatively.

Children know that:

Animals and plants can be grouped by simple observable features like size, number of legs, fish scales or shape of leaf.

Animals of the same species can show different physical characteristics (e.g. people with blue eyes or brown eyes are both humans/snails can have different patterns on their shells).

Children are able to:

Describe key factors as reasons for sorting animals and plants into groups.

Compare different common characteristics like shape, size of leaf.

Compare length/shape using non-standard measurements and record results in a prepared chart (e.g. weight of different seed types).

Make simple predictions about what they might observe.

Offer explanations for their observations and for simple patterns in recorded data, e.g. woodlice prefer dark, damp conditions.

Begin to organise and classify information using ICT and present their findings.

Enter, save and retrieve work.

Share ideas and co-operate with others.

Children know that:

There are physical characteristics that make the organism best suited to its environment, such as the gills on fish or the colour of insects.

There are physical characteristics shared by different species (e.g. all fish have fins, but there are still differences in size and colour between both different kinds of animals (i.e. sharks and sardines) and individuals of the same species).

Children are able to:

Ask questions, respond to suggestions and with help, seek answers to these questions.

Make simple predictions, e.g. about where woodlice would prefer to be.   *cont.*

Make simple SI measurements of length, height and mass, enter results in tables and write about them.

Interpret and explain the patterns they observe in results and investigations.

Use simple scientific vocabulary in a meaningful context (e.g. conditions, camouflage).

Use ICT to save information and to find and use appropriate stored information.

Use ICT to generate, develop, organise and present their work.

Co-operate with others (e.g. in caring for living things in the classroom).

Show an open-minded attitude to other people's ideas.

Children know that:

Animals can be grouped by observable characteristics such as number of legs, wings, gills, etc. so they can classify simple animals into groups such as insects, fish, birds, etc.

Organisms can be sorted into simple groups using a simple key.

Children are able to:

Plan and carry out an investigation using an approach that is as fair as possible (e.g. testing different woodlice habitats: light and dry, light and damp, dark and dry, dark and damp).

Use scientific equipment safely and appropriately.

Make a series of observations and measurements in seeking answers to questions.

Offer predictions based on prior experience and observations.

Offer explanations for perceived patterns, using scientific language as appropriate (e.g. many insects are camouflaged in the environment to avoid being eaten by predators).

Suggest reasons for and ways of improving their work.

Use a variety of sources, including ICT, to seek information.

Use ICT in a variety of ways to record and present information to an audience.

Show a reflective, open-minded attitude to themselves and others.

Table 4: Progression of Significant Attainment

Life processes and living things – Living things in the environment
Scientific enquiry skills and attitudes, ICT skills

Context

- Animals and plants can be found in different environments, and the conditions found in an environment affect the success of animals and plants living there.
- Food chains are an indication of the relationships between animals and plants in an ecosystem, and nearly all food chains start with green plants.

Concepts

- Living things live by feeding off the environment.
- Living things die and decay is a natural process.

Vocabulary and SI units

animal, autumn, bird, carnivore, conditions, environment, fish, flower, food, food chain, germinate, grow, habitat, herbivore, insect, leaf, light, mammal, natural, offspring, oxygen, plant, predator, prey, reproduce, roots, seeds, spring, summer, survive, temperature, tree, water, weather, winter

Progression of Learning Outcomes

Children know that:
Animals and plants are different.

They can identify some of the common plants and animals around them (e.g. oak, grass, bird, snail).

Children are able to:
Describe simply how animals/humans change as they grow.

Describe the observed physical differences between different humans by talking or record by pictures/simple charts.

Explore sources of information, including ICT, and talk about this.

Work co-operatively in measuring each other's height, foot length.

Children know that:
Plants and animals die.

Plants and animals need particular conditions to survive and link this to the fact that they are found in different environments (e.g. near water, under hedges).

Children are able to:
Make comparisons of different plants and animals in a nearby environment. *cont.*

Compare features using non-standard measurements and record in prepared charts.

Make simple predictions about what they might observe (e.g. animals sheltering on or under trees).

Offer explanations for their observations (e.g. there is a link between plant colour and smell and visiting animals).

Begin to organise and classify information using ICT and present their findings.

Share ideas and co-operate with others (e.g. in measuring each other).

Children know that:

They can identify characteristics that make the living thing adapted to its environment, e.g. colour of the animal for camouflage.

Children are able to:

Ask questions, respond to suggestions and, with help, seek answers to these questions.

Make simple predictions about which animals and plants will be found locally.

Explain the patterns they observe in results and investigations (e.g. insects are drawn to flowers by colour and smell to collect nectar).

Use simple scientific vocabulary in a meaningful context (e.g. habitat).

Use ICT to save information and to find and use appropriate stored information.

Use ICT to generate, develop, organise and present their work.

Co-operate with others.

Show an open-minded attitude to other people's ideas.

Children know that:

Animals feed on plants or other animals.

There is a relationship between plants and animals in a habitat, such as 'prey' and 'predator'.

Children are able to:

Plan and carry out an investigation using an approach that is as fair as possible (e.g. indoor snail habitats).

Use scientific equipment safely and appropriately (e.g. pooters, microscopes).

Make a series of observations and measurements in seeking answers to questions.

Offer predictions based on prior experience and observations.   *cont.*

Offer explanations for perceived patterns, using scientific language as appropriate (e.g. animals in the environment are prey or predator/herbivores or carnivores).

Suggest reasons for and ways of improving their work.

Use a variety of sources, including ICT, to seek information.

Use ICT in a variety of ways to record and present information to an audience.

Show a reflective, open-minded attitude to themselves and others.

Table 5: Progression of Significant Attainment

Materials and their properties – Classifying, grouping materials

Scientific enquiry skills and attitudes, ICT skills

Context

- Compare materials on the basis of their properties and how those properties relate to everyday uses of the materials (e.g. paper, fabrics).

- Materials can be grouped as solids, liquids and gases and each of these states have characteristics particular to them (e.g. ice, water, water vapour).

Concepts

- Materials can be grouped or classified according to their properties and those properties determine the uses the materials are put to.

- Materials can change and those changes can be either reversible or non-reversible.

- Materials can be separated by physical means.

Vocabulary and SI units

absorb, air, bend, boil, condensation, condense, conduct, conduction, cool, dissolve, dull, elastic, evaporate, filter, flexible, float, freeze, gas, heat, insoluble, liquid, material, melt, man-made, natural, rigid, rock, shiny, sieve, sink, soil, solid, substance, surface, temperature, thermometer, water vapour

Progression of Learning Outcomes

Children know that:

Things are made from materials and they can name some of the common materials around them, e.g. fabric, plastic.

Materials are chosen to do different jobs according to their properties, e.g. paper for absorbency, texture and colour for clothing, weight and strength for a cardboard box.

cont.

Children are able to:

Describe materials in simple terms: shiny, dull, coloured, hard, soft.

Describe the differences in different materials by talking or record by pictures/simple charts.

Explore sources of information, including ICT, and talk about what they found out.

Work co-operatively.

Children know that:

Different materials can be identified by their differences and similarities.

Materials can be sorted according to their common properties (e.g. texture, colour, weight, sources).

They can relate the properties of materials to simple uses of these materials.

Children are able to:

Describe key properties and simple comparisons that help them to identify those materials.

Use non-standard measurements to compare the properties of materials (e.g. cupfuls) and record in prepared charts.

Make simple predictions about what they might observe.

Offer explanations as to why certain materials are used for certain functions.

Begin to organise and classify information using ICT and present their findings.

Share ideas and co-operate with others.

Children know that:

There are ways of grouping and regrouping materials according to their properties.

There are some materials grouped as metals, plastics, glass, solid, liquid, gas, etc.

Some materials are magnetic.

Some materials conduct electricity.

Children are able to:

Ask and respond to questions, e.g. investigating the right type of material to insulate an ice lolly.

Make simple predictions about which paper will absorb the most water.   *cont.*

Make simple SI measurements of capacity and temperature, enter results in tables and write about them.

Interpret and explain the patterns they observe in results and investigations (e.g. the best paper towel and why).

Use simple scientific vocabulary in a meaningful context (e.g. absorbent, heat, insulate).

Use ICT to save information and to find and use appropriate stored information.

Use ICT to generate, develop, organise and present their work.

Co-operate with others.

Show an open-minded attitude to other people's ideas.

Children know that:

Some materials are difficult to classify (e.g. powder, cornflour) as solid, liquid or gas.

Some materials dissolve in water – with stirring, heating or breaking into small bits.

Children are able to:

Plan and carry out an investigation (e.g. dissolving salt in water) using an approach that is as fair as possible, that is, knowing what they will keep the same and what they will change each time.

Use scientific equipment safely and appropriately (e.g. digital balance).

Make a series of observations and measurements in seeking answers to questions.

Offer predictions based on prior experience and observations (e.g. how much salt will dissolve in a given quantity of water).

Offer explanations for perceived patterns, using scientific language as appropriate.

Suggest reasons for and ways of improving their work (e.g. insulating the ice lollies more tightly against the air).

Use a variety of sources, including ICT, to seek information.

Use ICT in a variety of ways to record and present information to an audience.

Show a reflective, open-minded attitude to themselves and others.

Table 6: Progression of Significant Attainment

Materials and their properties – Changing materials

Scientific enquiry skills and attitudes, ICT skills

Context

- Materials can be changed by physical (melting, evaporating, dissolving) or chemical (cooking) events.
- Change of state from solid to liquid to vapour or gas is reversible.
- Burning/cooking is a non-reversible change.
- When materials mix they can change and produce new substances.

Concepts

- Materials can be grouped according to their properties.
- The use of a material is dependent upon its properties.
- Changes in materials are reversible or non-reversible.
- Chemical change results in the formation of new substances while a physical change results in a change in the appearance of the material.

Vocabulary and SI units

air, boil, burn, carbon dioxide, chemical, condensation, condense, cook, dissolve, evaporate, freezing, gas, heat, insoluble, liquid, material, melt, rigid, rust, solid, soluble, solution, solvent, substance, synthetic, temperature, thermometer, water vapour

Temperature: degrees Celsius (°C)

Progression of Learning Outcomes

Children know that:
There is a variety of common materials and they can describe their physical appearance.

Children are able to:
Describe simply the differences in appearance of some materials like an egg or batter before and after cooking.

Describe the observed physical differences between two different sets of cooking, e.g. porridge and pancakes, by talking or record by pictures/simple charts.

Explore sources of information and story books.

Work co-operatively sharing tasks and responsibility.

Children know that:

There are common household materials and they can describe the differences and similarities between them.

There are observable changes when things burn, melt, cook or freeze.

Children are able to:

Describe key factors like melting or cooking that make materials change.

Make comparisons of the way things change (e.g. ice melting, water evaporating).

Compare the way things change under different conditions (e.g. greater heat).

Make simple predictions about what they might observe.

Offer explanations for their observations (e.g. cooking makes a new material out of the original materials).

Begin to organise and classify information using ICT and present their findings.

Share ideas and co-operate with others.

Children know that:

Materials have describable properties and that these properties make them useful.

There are naturally occurring materials and synthetic materials which are made from raw materials.

Materials change – either reversibly or non-reversibly.

Simple materials can be sorted into solids, liquids and gases.

Children are able to:

Ask questions and investigate change: e.g. salt dissolving in water/heat in melting ice.

Make simple predictions about the time it will take for salt to evaporate from the solution.

Make simple SI measurements of time and capacity, enter results in tables and write about them.

Interpret and explain the patterns they observe in results and investigations.

Use simple scientific vocabulary in a meaningful context (e.g. soluble, solid, liquid).

Use ICT to save information and to find and use appropriate stored information.

Use ICT to generate, develop, organise and present their work.

Co-operate with others.

Show an open-minded attitude to other people's ideas.

Children know that:

Materials exist as solids, liquids or gases and solids can change to a liquid and liquid to a gas.

There are scientific names for physical changes, such as melt, boil, etc. and they can use these words in a meaningful way.

Children are able to:

Plan and carry out an investigation (e.g. dissolving or insulating a 'hot' cup of tea) using an approach that is as fair as possible.

Use scientific equipment safely and appropriately (e.g. balance, thermometer).

Make a series of observations and measurements in seeking answers to questions (e.g. melting or dissolving).

Offer predictions based on prior experience and observations.

Offer explanations for perceived patterns, using scientific language as appropriate (e.g. melt, solvent, dissolve, crystals).

Suggest reasons for and ways of improving their work.

Use a variety of sources, including ICT to seek information.

Use ICT in a variety of ways to record and present information to an audience.

Table 7: Progression of Significant Attainment

Materials and their properties – Separating mixtures of materials

Scientific enquiry skills and attitudes, ICT skills

Context

- Solid particles of different sizes can be separated by sieving (e.g. raisins and flour).
- Some solids dissolve to give solutions but some solids do not (e.g. salt, flour).
- Dissolved solids can be recovered by evaporation of the liquid.
- Some insoluble solids can be separated by filtering the solid from the liquid.
- There is a limit to the mass of solid that can dissolve in a given amount of water.

Concepts

- Materials can be grouped or classified according to their properties and those properties determine the uses the materials are put to.
- Materials can change and those changes can be either reversible or non-reversible.
- Materials can be separated by physical means.

Vocabulary and SI units

boil, burn, chemical, condensation, condense, colour, cook, dissolve, evaporate, evaporation, filter, freeze, gas, heat, insoluble, liquid, mass, material, mixture, melt, sediment, separate, solid, soluble, solution, solvent, substance, temperature, thermometer, water vapour

Progression of Learning Outcomes

Children know that:
There are observable changes which they can describe when salt is added to fresh water – the water becomes salty.

Children are able to:
Describe simply how the sieve stopped the lentils and raisins going through the sieve but not the salt or some of the flour.

Describe the observed physical differences, grain sizes of lentils, raisins and flour.

Explore sources of information, including ICT, and talk about this.

Work co-operatively.

Children know that:
Large particles stay in the filter or sieve when water is poured through; large particles cannot go through.

Some particles are so small that they go through the sieve.

When something is filtered, something has come out of the water.

Children are able to:
Use different size sieves to separate the different sized particles.

Use a magnet to separate magnetic objects from non-magnetic objects.

Recognise that different properties of materials allow for separation.

Make simple predictions about what they might observe when a salty solution is left standing overnight in a warm place.

Offer explanations for their observations and for simple patterns in recorded data (e.g. salt 're-appearing' from solution).

Begin to organise and classify information using ICT and present their findings.

Share ideas and co-operate with others.

Children know that:

There is a change in fresh water when we add salt.

A salt solution is made of different substances – the fresh water and dissolved salt.

Children are able to:

Ask questions, respond to suggestions and, with help, seek answers to these questions (e.g. how much salt will dissolve in a given set of water?).

Make simple predictions about the effect of stirring or heating on dissolving.

Make simple SI measurements of capacity and mass, enter results in tables and write about them.

Interpret and explain the patterns they observe in results and investigations.

Use simple scientific vocabulary in a meaningful context.

Use ICT to save information and to find and use appropriate stored information.

Co-operate with others.

Show an open-minded attitude to other people's ideas.

Children know that:

Materials can be separated by simple methods such as filtration or using magnets.

Stirring, heating or breaking materials into small bits can increase the rate of change.

Different solutes dissolve in different solvents; some materials are insoluble.

Children are able to:

Plan and carry out an investigation using an approach that is as fair as possible (e.g. separating chocolate bits from chocolate chip cookies).

Use scientific equipment safely and appropriately (e.g. handlenses, filters).

Make a series of observations and measurements in seeking answers to questions (e.g. if salt and other solutes dissolve in oil).

Offer predictions based on prior experience and observations.

Offer explanations for perceived patterns, using scientific language as appropriate (e.g. some materials are insoluble in oil or water).

Suggest reasons for and ways of improving their work.

Use a variety of sources, including ICT, to seek information.

Use ICT in a variety of ways to record and present information to an audience.

Show a reflective, open-minded attitude to themselves and others.

Table 8: Progression of Significant Attainment

Physical processes – Electricity

Scientific enquiry skills and attitudes, ICT skills

Context

- A complete circuit is needed and that would include a battery or power supply in order to make electrical devices work.
- The electricity flowing in a circuit can be controlled by varying the current or stopping the current by a switch.
- Electrical circuits can be represented by drawings and symbols.

Concepts

- Electricity flows in a circuit and can be used to do work.
- Electricity is a flow of charged particles.
- Materials have properties which allow electricity to flow easily or stop the electricity flowing.

Vocabulary and SI units

battery, bulb, buzzer, circuit, conduct, conductor, connect, current, electricity, energy, gap, light, motor, resist, switch, wire

Units: volts (v) = 'electrical push'

Progression of Learning Outcomes

Children know that:
A bulb will light up in an electrical circuit when the circuit is complete.

A switch can close a gap in a circuit and allow the electricity to flow.

Household electricity is dangerous.

Children are able to:
Describe simply what they see and what action lets a bulb light up in a simple electrical circuit.

Describe what happens in a circuit using speech, pictures or symbols.

Explore other devices such as buzzers.

Work co-operatively in creating working circuits.

Children know that:

A battery can be used to provide electricity for a circuit to work.

Different devices can be made to work with electricity.

Mains electricity must not be used for investigations on electricity.

Children are able to:

Describe different devices like bulbs or buzzers in circuits.

Compare bulb brightness or loudness of buzzers.

Make simple predictions about what might happen if there is a gap in the circuit.

Offer explanations for their observations when there is a gap in the circuit.

Share ideas and co-operate with others.

Children know that:

Metals allow electricity pass through them and these are called conductors.

Both poles of a battery must be connected in a circuit and the switch closed in order for the circuit to work.

If a circuit is broken and there is a gap, the bulb will not light up.

Children are able to:

Ask questions about what might happen if different materials are used to close the gap in a circuit.

Make simple predictions about the different materials used.

Interpret and explain the patterns they observe in results and investigations.

Use simple scientific vocabulary in a meaningful context (e.g. battery, switch).

Use electrical circuits in a problem-solving activity.

Co-operate with others.

Show an open-minded attitude to other people's ideas.

Children know that:

Electrical batteries, devices and wires can be represented by drawings or symbols.

Some materials conduct electricity well and some materials resist the flow of electricity.

Batteries have two different poles.   *cont.*

> *Children are able to:*
>
> Use electricity to plan, design and make a warning system using circuits, bulbs and buzzers.
>
> Use electrical equipment safely and appropriately.
>
> Offer predictions about lighting up based on prior experience and observations.
>
> Offer explanations for how a switch works and the nature of insulators/conductors.
>
> Suggest reasons for and ways of improving their designs.
>
> Use ICT in a variety of ways to record and present information to an audience.
>
> Show a reflective, open-minded attitude to themselves and others.

Table 9: Progression of Significant Attainment

Physical processes – Forces and motion

Scientific enquiry skills and attitudes, ICT skills

Context

- Describe movement and the forces acting when things move.
- Develop the idea that forces are pushes and pulls and they cause changes in materials and the speed with which things move.
- The idea of balanced and unbalanced forces to explain why things stay still (in equilibrium) or move in different directions at different speeds.
- Magnetism and gravity are two forces.
- Objects float when the downward force is less than the upthrust from the water.

Concepts

- Forces are pushes and pulls and can act on a body to cause changes in its position, rate of movement or the shape of the object.
- Forces act in pairs so there is opposition to the action of a force.
- Gravity is an attracting force associated with the Earth and is responsible for weight.
- Magnetism is a force associated with particular materials, electricity and the Earth.

Vocabulary and SI units

air resistance, anti-clockwise, attract, balance, bend, clockwise, density, direction, equilibrium, flexible, float, force, friction, gravity, grip, magnet, magnetism, pole (north and south), prediction, push, pull, repel, resist, rigid, speed, twist, unbalanced, weight

Progression of Learning Outcomes

Children know that:

An object can change when a force pushes or pulls it.

Things with wheels move easier than things without wheels.

Objects can be made to balance or remain 'at rest'.

Children are able to:

Describe simply how two toys move when pushed (e.g. a toy car on a ramp, a boat in water).

Describe the observed reactions of different moving toys by talking or record by pictures/simple charts.

Work co-operatively.

Children know that:

If we want to move an object we have to give it a push or pull it.

If we want to make the object move faster, we have to push harder or drop it from a greater height.

If we want to stop an object we put something in its way or make it change direction by pushing more on one side.

Two magnets can push or pull each other.

Children are able to:

Describe key factors that help an object stay still or move further.

Make comparisons of the movement of different toys.

Compare distance travelled and other features using non-standard measurements and record in prepared charts.

Make simple predictions about what they might observe (e.g. when different quantities of modelling clay are used).

Offer explanations for their observations and for simple patterns in recorded data (e.g. a rough ramp slows down a toy car/less clay lowers stability).

Begin to organise and classify information using ICT and present their findings.

Enter, save and retrieve work.

Share ideas and co-operate with others.

Children know that:

An object moving will soon stop – it can't go on moving forever.

Heavy objects need a big force to move them.

Light or round objects need a smaller force to move them.

Large light or hollow objects full of air float in water.

Forces can be represented by pictures or symbols (an arrow).

Force is measured in Newtons.

A magnet has poles and like poles repel; unlike poles attract.

Children are able to:

Ask questions, respond to suggestions and, with help, seek answers to these questions (e.g. will more modelling clay make the sledge move further? faster?).

Make simple predictions about their investigations.

Make simple SI measurements of length, depth and mass, enter results in tables and write about them.

Interpret and explain the patterns they observe in results and investigations (e.g. why some objects float and others do not).

Use simple scientific vocabulary in a meaningful context (e.g. force, distance, speed).

Use ICT to save information and to find and use appropriate stored information.

Use ICT to generate, develop, organise and present their work.

Co-operate with others in collecting and recording data.

Show an open-minded attitude to other people's ideas.

Children know that:

Forces have strength and direction.

An object will move in the same direction as the greater pushing or pulling force.

Forces act in pairs – an opposite force to the applied force (e.g. change in speed of movement depends upon the size of the applied force/floating objects are less dense than an equal volume of water).

Objects at rest have forces in equilibrium.

Weight = a force of gravity. Mass = a quantity of matter.

Children are able to:

Plan and carry out an investigation using an approach that is as fair as possible.

Use scientific equipment safely and appropriately (e.g. Newtonmeters).   *cont.*

Make a series of observations and measurements in seeking answers to questions (weight of clay and its effect on equilibrium).

Offer predictions based on prior experience and observations.

Offer explanations for perceived patterns, using scientific language as appropriate.

Suggest reasons for and ways of improving their work.

Use a variety of sources, including ICT, to seek information.

Use ICT in a variety of ways to record and present information to an audience.

Show a reflective, open-minded attitude to themselves and others.

Table 10: Progression of Significant Attainment

Physical processes – Light and sound

Scientific enquiry skills and attitudes, ICT skills

Context

- Light travels from a source and we see because light enters our eyes.
- In the absence of light we cannot see.
- Light is unable to pass through some materials, causing shadows; other surfaces reflect light.
- White light is made up of different wavelengths of coloured light.
- Sound is made by vibrations which travel through a variety of materials to reach the ear, but not all the vibrations are heard.
- Pitch and loudness of sounds can be changed.

Concepts

- Light comes from luminous sources.
- Sound comes from vibrating objects.
- Light and sound are different kinds of wave.
- Light and sound appear to travel in straight lines and interact with materials.

Vocabulary and SI units

absorb, colour, dark, direction, ear, echo, eye, kaleidoscope, light, loudness, material, mirror, nocturnal, opaque, periscope, pitch, reflect, reflection, shadow, shiny, sound, source, sun, surface, transparent, vibrate, vibrations

Progression of Learning Outcomes

> *Children know that:*
> There are different common sources of light and sound around them.
>
> *Children are able to:*
> Describe simply the sources of light and sounds around them.
> Describe the different colours around them and in the living environment.
> Work co-operatively.

> *Children know that:*
> Different sources of light can be compared in terms of similarities and
> differences (e.g. colour and brightness).
> Different sources of sound can be compared in terms of similarities and
> differences (e.g. loudness or pitch).
>
> *Children are able to:*
> Make comparisons of different sounds or level of brightness in sources of light.
> Put in order sounds, colours and light using non-standard measurements and
> record in prepared charts.
> Make simple predictions about what sounds and colours they might observe in
> the living environment.
> Offer explanations for their observations and for simple patterns (e.g. light and
> shadows, different materials in sound makers).
> Begin to organise and classify information using ICT, and present their findings.
> Share ideas and co-operate with others.

> *Children know that:*
> There are reasons why sometimes sounds can get fainter and light gets dimmer
> and they can make general statements about this.
> In certain conditions, shadows are formed and light is reflected.
> Certain colours act as camouflage in the environment.
>
> *Children are able to:*
> Ask questions, respond to suggestions and, with help, seek answers to these
> questions (e.g. what shadows are formed when objects are placed at
> different distances from the light source).
> Make simple predictions about the most effective colours for camouflage. *cont.*

Make simple SI measurements of length and enter results in tables and write about them.

Interpret and explain the patterns they observe in results and investigations.

Use simple scientific vocabulary in a meaningful context (reflection, vibration).

Use ICT to save information and to find and use appropriate stored information.

Use ICT to generate, develop, organise and present their work.

Co-operate with others.

Show an open-minded attitude to other people's ideas.

Children know that:

There are causes of shadows, echoes and reflections and can describe these.

There is a relationship between the characteristics of a shadow and the object, the position of light and the strength of light.

Sound is caused by vibrations.

Light appears to travel in straight lines while sound appears to travel in all directions.

Certain colours are used by humans to warn of dangers ahead.

Children are able to:

Plan and carry out an investigation using an approach that is as fair as possible (e.g. the effect of different lengths and strengths of elastic bands in sound boxes).

Use scientific equipment safely and appropriately (e.g. mirrors, tuning forks).

Make a series of observations and measurements in seeking answers to questions.

Offer predictions based on prior experience and observations.

Offer explanations for perceived patterns, using scientific language as appropriate (reflection, vibration).

Suggest reasons for and ways of improving their work (e.g. more accurate measurement).

Use a variety of sources, including ICT, to seek information.

Use ICT in a variety of ways to record and present information to an audience.

Show a reflective, open-minded attitude to themselves and others.

Bibliography

Association for Science Education (ASE) (2000) *Be Safe! Some Aspects of Safety in School Science and Technology for Key Stage 1 and 2.* Hatfield: ASE.

Barnes, D., Britton, J. and Torbe, M. (1986 edition) *Language, The Learner and The School.* London: Penguin.

Bloom, B. S. (1956) *Taxonomy of Educational Objectives, Volume 1.* London: Longman.

de Bóo, M. (1999) *Enquiring Children, Challenging Teaching.* Buckingham: Open University Press.

British Association National Science Week. Available at: the-ba.org.uk/nsw

Bruner, J. S. (1968) *The Processes of Cognitive Growth: Infancy.* Clark University Press: USA.

Bruner, J. S. and Haste, H. (eds) (1993 edition) *Making Sense: The Child's Construction of the World.* London: Methuen.

Cosgrove, J. M. and Patterson, C. J. (1977) *Plans and the Development of Listener Skills.* New York: Basic Books.

Department for Education and Employment (DfEE) (1997) *Excellence in Schools.* London: DfEE.

Department for Education and Employment (DfEE)/Qualifications and Curriculum Authority (QCA) (1998) *Scheme of Work for Key Stages 1 and 2.* London: DfEE/QCA.

Department for Education and Employment (DfEE)/Qualifications and Curriculum Authority (QCA) (1999) *The National Curriculum: Handbook for Primary Teachers in England, Key Stages 1 and 2.* London: DfEE/QCA.

Donaldson, M. (1987 edition) *Children's Minds.* London: Fontana Press.

Fisher, R. (1994 edition) *Teaching Children to Think.* Hemel Hempstead: Simon and Schuster.

Galton, M. J., Simon, B. and Croll, P. (1980) *Inside the Primary Classroom.* London: Routledge and Kegan Paul.

Keogh, B. and Naylor, S., de Bóo, M. and Barnes, J. (2002) *PGCE Professional Workbook: Primary Science.* Exeter: Learning Matters.

Koshy, V. (2002) *Teaching Gifted Children 4–7.* London: David Fulton Publishers.

Lifelong Learning Foundation/Bayliss, V. (2000) *What Should our Children Learn?* In Campaign for learning, RSA.

Merry, R. (1998) *Successful Children, Successful Teaching.* Buckingham: Open University Press.

Naylor, S. and Keogh, B. (2000) *Concept Cartoons in Science Education.* Sandbach: Millgate House Publishers.

O'Brien, P. (1998) *Teaching Scientifically Able Pupils in the Primary School.* Oxford: NACE (National Association for Able Children in Education).

Office for Standards in Education (Ofsted) (1993) *First Class.* London: Ofsted.

Office for Standards in Education (Ofsted) (1994) *Exceptionally Able Children. Report of Conferences.* London: Ofsted.

Qualter, A. (1996) *Differentiated Primary Science.* Buckingham: Open University Press.

Redfield, D. L. and Rousseau, E. W. (1981) 'A meta-analysis of experimental research on teacher questioning behaviour', *Review of Educational Research* **51**, 237–45.

Robinson, E. J. and Robinson, W. P. (1981) 'Ways of reacting to communication failure in relation to the development of the child's understanding about verbal communication', *European Journal of Social Psychology* **11**, 189–208.

Russell, T., Black, P., Harlen, W. *et al.* (1988) *Science at Age 11: A Review of APU Findings 1980–84.* London: HMSO.

Scottish Office Education Department (2000) *Curriculum and Assessment Scotland National Guidelines: Environmental Studies 5–14.* Edinburgh: Scottish Office Educational Department.

Silverman, L. (1993) *Counselling the Gifted and Talented.* Colorado: Love Publishing.

Stringer, J./SATIS (Science and Technology in Society) (1996) *SATIS Resources 5–8 and 8–14.* Hatfield: ASE. Available at: www.ase.org.uk

Sylva, K. (1994) 'The impact of early learning on children's later development', in *Start Right: The Importance of Early Learning, x–y.* London: Royal Society of Arts.

Tizard, B. and Hughes, M. (1984) *Young Children Learning.* London: Fontana.

Vygotsky, L. (1986 edition) *Thought and Language.* Massachusetts: Massachusetts Institute of Technology.

Wood, D. (1992 edition) *How Children Think and Learn.* Oxford: Blackwell Publishers.

Useful Resources

Books about the teaching of science

Association for Science Education (ASE) (2000) *Be Safe! Some Aspects of Safety in School Science and Technology for Key Stage 1 and 2.* Hatfield: ASE.

de Bóo, M. (1999) *Enquiring Children, Challenging Teaching.* Buckingham: Open University Press.

Farrow, S. (1996) *The Really Useful Science Book: A Framework of Knowledge for Primary Teachers.* London: Falmer Press.

Feasey, R. (1998) *Primary Science Equipment.* Hatfield: ASE.

Feasey, R. (1999) *Primary Science and Literacy Links.* Hatfield: ASE.

Feasey, R. and Gallear, B. (2000) *Primary Science and Numeracy.* Hatfield: ASE.

Feasey, R. and Gallear, B. (2001) *Primary Science and Information Communication Technology.* Hatfield: ASE. (includes useful CD-ROM)

Feasey, R. and Goldsworthy, A. (revised by Ball, S.) (1997) *Making Sense of Primary Science Investigations.* Hatfield: ASE.

Frost, R. (1993) *The IT in Primary Science Book.* Hatfield: ASE.

Harlen, W. (1992) *The Teaching of Science in Primary Schools.* London: David Fulton Publishers.

Selley, N. (1999) *The Art of Constructivist Teaching in the Primary School.* London: David Fulton Publishers.

Sherrington, R. (1998) *ASE Guide to Primary Science Education.* Hatfield: Association for Science Education/Stanley Thornes.

Books with science activities and/or information

D'Amico, J. and Drummond, K. E. (1995) *The Science Chef: 100 Fun Food Experiments and Recipes.* New York: John Wiley and Sons.

de Bóo, M. (1996 edition) *Action Rhymes and Games.* Leamington Spa: Scholastic.

de Bóo, M. (2004) *Nature Detectives: Environmental Science for Primary Children.* Hatfield: ASE/Woodland Trust.

Burgess, L. (1996) *Cooking Activities. Bright Ideas for Early Years*. Leamington Spa: Scholastic.

Godfrey, S. (1993) *Environmental Activities*. Leamington Spa: Scholastic Publications.

Matusiak, C. (1994 edition) *Seasonal Activities: Spring and Summer; Autumn and Winter*. Leamington Spa: Scholastic.

Naylor, S. and Keogh, B. (2000) *Concept Cartoons in Science Education*. Sandbach: Millgate House Publishers. (book, posters and children's science story books)

Oakes, M. (ed.) (1996) *Investigating the Environment at KS1 and KS2*. Hatfield: ASE.

Parkin, T. and Lewis, M. (eds) (1998) *Science and Literacy: A Guide for Primary Teachers*. London: Nuffield/Collins Educational.

Pattinson, J. (2000) *Schools Organic Gardens*. Hatfield: ASE.

Richards, R. (1990) *An Early Start to Technology*. Hemel Hempstead: Simon and Schuster.

Richards, R. (1991) *An Early Start to Ourselves and Evolution*. Hemel Hempstead: Simon and Schuster.

Richards, R. (1992) *An Early Start to Energy*. Hemel Hempstead: Simon and Schuster.

Richards, R. (1992) *The Primary Teacher's Reference Book of Metals*. Hemel Hempstead: Simon and Schuster.

Sanders, D. (1999) *Plants in their Environment: KS1/Prim. 1–3*. Leamington Spa: Scholastic.

Smith, G. (1990 onwards) *5–13 Electricity: Making it Work*. Hertford: MSTEC (Middlesex Science and Technology Centre).

(1993) *Projects for Science and Technology with Music*. London: Watts and Questions Publishing.

Poetry books to inspire science

Collins (1989) *Mother Goose Nursery Rhymes* (traditional rhymes). Collins.

Feasey, R. (ed.) *Science is like a Tub of Ice Cream: Cool and Fun, A Collection of 100 Science Poems by Primary and Secondary School Children*. ASE.

Foster, J. (compiler) *Twinkle, Twinkle, Chocolate Bar: Rhymes for the Very Young*. Oxford University Press.

Foster, J. and Thompson, C. *Bedtime Rhymes*. Oxford University Press.

Milne, A. A. *Now We Are Six*. Methuen.

Milne, A. A. *When We Were Very Young*. Methuen.

Books of songs to inspire science

Bird, W., Evans, D. and McAuliffe, G. (eds) *Sing a Song One*. Nelson. *Someone's Singing Lord*. A & C Black.

Harrop, B. (ed.) *Apusskidu*. A & C Black.

Harrop, B. (ed.) *Okki Tokki Unga*. A & C Black.

Stories for children with relevance for science

Armitage, D. and Armitage, R. *The Lighthouse Keeper's Lunch*. Scholastic Children's Books.

Barrie, J. M. *Peter Pan*. London: Puffin Classics.

The Big Pancake. retold by N. Baxter. Ladybird Books.

Burningham, J. *The Car Ride*. Walker Books.

Briggs, R. *The Snowman*. London: Puffin Books.

Carle, E. *The Bad-tempered Ladybird*. Picture Puffin.

Carle, E. *The Very Hungry Caterpillar*. Picture Puffin.

Carle, E. *The Very Lonely Firefly*. Hamish Hamilton.

Clarke, M. and Voake, C. *The Very Best of Aesop's Fables*. Walker Books.

Curry, P. *The Big Red Bus Ride*. Picture Lions.

Dr Seuss. *One Fish, Two Fish, Red Fish, Blue Fish*. Beginner Books.

Edminston, J. *The Emperor Who Hated Yellow*. Barefoot Beginners.

Edwards, D. *My Naughty Little Sister*. Young Puffin.

Gibbs, L. (translator) 'How the sea became salty' in *Aesop's Fables*. Oxford World Classics. Oxford University Press.

Grant, G. and Hellard, S. *Little Blue Car*. Orchard Books.

Gribbin, M. and Tewson, A. *Big Bugs*. Ladybird.

Hodgeson Burnett, F. *The Secret Garden*. Puffin.

Hughes, S. *Out and About*. Walker Books.

Hutchins, P. *Don't Forget the Bacon*. Picture Puffin.

Hutchins, P. *The Wind Blew*. Red Fox Picture Books.

Hutchins, P. *Titch*. Red Fox Books.

Inkpen, M. *Kipper's Birthday*. Picture Knights.

Kerr, J. *The Tiger Who Came to Tea*. Picture Lions.

Ladybird. *Goldilocks and the Three Bears*. Ladybird Easy Reading Books.

Ladybird. *The Elves and the Shoemaker*. Ladybird Easy Reading Books.

Ladybird. *The Little Gingerbread Boy*. Ladybird Easy Reading Books.

Ladybird. *The Little Red Hen and the Grains of Wheat*. Ladybird Easy Reading Books.

Ladybird. *The Magic Porridge Pot*. Ladybird Easy Reading Books.

Ladybird. *The Three Billy Goats Gruff*. Ladybird Easy Reading Books.

Ladybird. *The Three Little Pigs and the Big Bad Wolf*. Ladybird Easy Reading Books.

Lester, H. and Munsinger, L. *Me First*. Macmillan.

MacDonald, A. and Fox-Davies, S. *Little Beaver and The Echo*. Walker Books.

Mckee, D. *Elmer*. Red Fox Picture Books.

Moray Williams, U. *The Adventures of Little Wooden Horse*. Young Puffin.

Morris, N. and Stevenson, P. *Feel!* Firefly Books.

Richardson, J. and Englander, A. *Tall Inside*. Picture Puffins.

Rockwell, A. *Bikes*. Picture Puffin.

Roffey, M. *What's the Weather?* Macmillan.

Rosen, M. and Oxenbury, H. *We're Going on a Bear Hunt* (sounds). Walker Books.

Rowan, P. *The Amazing Voyage of the Cucumber Sandwich*. Jonathan Cape.

Sendak, M. *Where the Wild Things are*. Picture Lions.

Stewart, K. and Shepard, E. H. *The Pooh Cook Book*. Magnet Books.

Stoll Walsh, E. *Mouse Paint*. Orchard Books.

Tomlinson, J. *The Owl who was Afraid of the Dark*. Young Puffin.

Traditional. *Jack and the Beanstalk*. Picture Puffin.

Traditional. *Snow White and the Seven Dwarves*. Benwig Books.

Traditional. *The Musicians of Bremen*. Benwig Books.

Vyner, T. *The Tree*. Collins Picture Lions.

Watson, C. *Aesop's Fables*. Usborne Publishing.

Yeoman, J. and Blake, Q. *The Do-It-Yourself House that Jack Built*. Puffin.

Zolotow, C. and Sendak, M. *Mr Rabbit and the Lovely Present* (colours). Picture Puffin.

Information books for children to read, research and enjoy

Ardley, B. and Ardley, N. *The A–Z of the Human Body* (Oxford Children's Books). Oxford University Press.

Bright, M. *World About Us* series (including *Traffic Pollution; Polluting the Oceans*). Gloucester Press.

Burnie, D. *Eyewitness Guides: Plant*. Dorling Kindersley.

Burnie, D. *Eyewitness Guides: Tree*. Dorling Kindersley.

Evans, D. and Williams, C. *Magnets and Batteries. Let's Explore Science Books*. Dorling Kindersley.

Ganeri, A. *I Wonder Why the Wind Blows . . . and other questions*. Kingfisher.

Hewitt, S. *Get Set Go!* series on science and music (including *Puff and Blow; Bang and Rattle; Pluck and Scrape; Squeak and Roar*). Franklin Watts.

Hooper, R. *Life in the Woodlands. Jump! Ecology Books*. Two-Can.

Janulewicz, M. *Yikes! Your body, up CLOSE!* Collins Children's Books.

Ladybird. *Big Ocean Creatures*. Ladybird.

Ladybird. *Big Bugs*. Ladybird First Discovery Books.

Llewellyn, C. *The Seasons: Topic Box*. Wayland.

Marshall, D. *Facts at your Fingertips* series (including *The Atmosphere; The Earth*; and *The Sea*). Simon and Schuster.

Morgan, S. *Mini-beasts: Topic Box*. Wayland.

Morris, J. *The Animal Roundabout* (life cycles). Dorling Kindersley.

Moss, M. *The Weather in Winter*. Wayland.

Pluckrose, H. *Floating and Sinking. Think About Books*. Franklin Watts.

Poole, S. *Mini-beasts Photo Pack*. Folens Science.

Qualter, A. and Quinn, J. *Look After Yourself: Healthy Food*. Wayland.

Sneddon, R. *What is a Fish?* Belitha Press.

Sneddon, R. *What is a Flower?* Belitha Press.

Stringer, J. *Fourways Farm: Floating and Sinking* (and other books). Macdonald Young Books and Channel 4. (highly recommended TV series)

Tanner, G. and Wood, T. *History Mysteries Books* series (including *Cleaning; Eating; Farming*; and *In the Street*). A & C Black.

Taylor, B. *Sound and Music: Science Starters*. Franklin Watts.

Thompson, R. *How it's Made: Pencils*. Watts.

Wood, J. *Storms. Jump! Nature Book*. Two-Can.

Woolfitt, G. *Science through the Seasons: Spring*. Wayland.

Yates, I. and Austin, G. *From Birth to Death: Life Cycles*. Belitha Press.

Websites

ASE: www.ase.org.uk

BBC (TV weather forecasts): www.bbc.co.uk/weather

British Association for the Advancement of Science (activities and events for children and adults, especially National Science Week): www.the-ba.net/nsw

Buglife – The Invertebrate Conservation Trust: www.buglife.org.uk

Concept Cartoons: www.conceptcartoons.com

Dorling Kindersley Education Software: www.brainworks.co.uk

Explore Museum: www.exploratorium.edu

Flora for Fauna (Natural History Museum): Email: fff@nhm.ac.uk

Learning through Landscapes: www.ltl.org.uk

National Grid for Learning: www.ngfl.gov.uk

Natural History Museum: www.nhm.ac.uk

Phenology Project (the study of Nature's calendar): www.phenology.org.uk

Primary Investigations: www.science.org.acu/pi

Primary Resources: www.primaryresources.co.uk

Teaching Ideas: www.teachingideas.co.uk

The Big Bug Show: www.thebigbugshow.demon.co.uk

The Met Office (weather): www.metoffice.com

The Science Museum: www.nmsi.ac.uk/welcome.html

The Woodland Trust (and the interactive CD-ROM *Wild about Woods*): www.woodland-trust.org.uk

Tivola 2000 CD-ROM series *Oscar the Balloonist*: www.tivola.co.uk

Wild Flower Society (Identify plants, take part in surveys): www.schoolzone.co.uk

Suppliers of science equipment and ICT resources

5–13 Electricity – Constructional Kits

5–13 Energy Packs, PO Box 513, Hertford, SG14 3PH

Anglia Multimedia 'Garden Life', 'Seashore Life': www.granada-learning.com

Data Harvest Group Ltd (especially good for child-friendly sensing devices)

Woburn Lodge, Waterloo Road, Linslade, Leighton Buzzard, Bedfordshire, LU7 7NR

Dorling Kindersley (good CD-ROMs of graphing programs, children's encyclopaedia, investigating the human body, etc.), e.g. 'Encyclopedia of Nature'

1 Horsham Gates, North Street, Horsham, West Sussex RH13 5PJ

Electricity Association Services Ltd (Understanding Electricity Educational Service)

30 Millbank, London SW1 4RD

Philip Harris Education (good science equipment)

Movora House, Ashby Park, Ashby de la Zouch, Leicestershire, LE5 1NG

Research Machines Education Software ('Easiteach Science', 'Starting Graph 1.5')

Unit 140, Milton Park, Abingdon, OX14 4SE

Sherston Software (Clip Art, etc.) Swan Barton, Sherston, Malmesbury, Wilts. SN16 0LH

TTS Group Ltd, Educational Supplies (good science equipment)

Nunn Brook Road, Huthwaite, Sutton in Ashfield, Nottinghamshire, NG17 2HU

Tel: 01623 447 800

Website: www.tts-group.co.uk

Yorkshire International/Thomson Multimedia Limited

The Television Centre, Kirkstall Road, Leeds LE56 1JS

Index